THE
NATION TAKES SHAPE
1789–1837

The Natio

THE CHICAGO HISTORY OF AMERICAN CIVILIZATION

Daniel J. Boorstin, EDITOR

Takes Shape: 1789-1837

By Marcus Cunliffe

 THE UNIVERSITY OF CHICAGO PRESS

CHICAGO AND LONDON

Library of Congress Catalog Card Number: 59-5770

THE UNIVERSITY OF CHICAGO PRESS, CHICAGO & LONDON
The University of Toronto Press, Toronto 5, Canada

© *1959 by The University of Chicago. Published 1959*
Seventh Impression 1965. Printed in the United States of
America

Editor's Preface

In recent years, we have become more than ever self-conscious in quest of our national character. Social scientists have used the specialized tools of sociology, psychology, and economics to describe what is characteristically American. But our historians have long been engaged in this search. In their attempts to portray the many-sidedness of life in America, they have been helping us discover ourselves.

Mr. Cunliffe, in his account of the first half-century (1789–1837) of life under the federal Constitution, sees an American character emerging as the new nation expanded across the continent. He shows us how colonials began to become Americans, how a new nation found itself. He uses his lively narrative not only to describe a people making its own way but to warn us against tempting oversimplifications. In the critical years between the adoption of the Constitution and the end of the presidency of Andrew Jackson, he clearly discerns a number of strong and conflicting tendencies—among others, the conflict between city and countryside, between the nation and the region, between conservatism and experimentalism. He finds what is characteristically American not in the emergence of a few simple and permanent features but in a peculiar and continuing tension among contending forces.

For his use of our history to help us discover ourselves, Mr. Cunliffe is well fitted, not only from his familiarity with the documents of that age but also because he was educated in England and has lived most of his life there. He has the special advantage of one who stands at a friendly distance. With this book he puts himself in the company of the perceptive and articulate visitors from abroad who, since the early nineteenth century, have been discovering things about us which we might not have been able to discover for ourselves.

The "Chicago History of American Civilization" aims to bring to the general reader, in compact and readable form, the insights of scholars who write from different points of view. This series contains two kinds of books: a *chronological* group, which will provide a coherent narrative of American history from its beginning to the present day, and a *topical* group, which will deal with the history of varied and significant aspects of American life. Twenty-odd titles in the series are in preparation. Those which have already been published are listed at the end of this volume. Mr. Cunliffe's book—one of the chronological group—picks up the story where it was left by Edmund S. Morgan's *The Birth of the Republic: 1763–1789.*

DANIEL J. BOORSTIN

Table of Contents

I

"Half a Century of Progress"

In 1841 a distinguished American cleric, scholar, and reformer who was then in his early sixties gave a talk in Philadelphia. The man was William Ellery Channing; the theme of his address was "The Present Age"; and in the course of his lecture he cast a look back at the previous age:

In the period through which many of us have passed what thrones have been shaken! what hearts have bled! what millions have been butchered by their fellow-creatures! what hopes of philanthropy have been blighted! And, at the same time, what magnificent enterprises have been achieved! what new provinces won to science and art! what rights and liberties secured to nations! It is a privilege to have lived in an age so stirring, so pregnant, so eventful. It is an age never to be forgotten. . . . Its impression on history is indelible. Amidst its events the American Revolution, the first distinct, solemn assertion of the rights of men, and the French Revolution, that volcanic force which shook the earth to its centre, are never to pass from men's minds.

It had been, Channing thought, an age of giants, with George Washington, Benjamin Franklin, and Napoleon Bonaparte preeminent. But there was "something greater in the age than its greatest men; it is the appearance of a new power in the world, the appearance of a multitude of men on that stage where as yet the few have acted their parts alone."

Revolution, nationalism, and democracy were, then, among the major themes of Channing's lifetime as he saw it in retrospect. Change was the universal rule. In 1789, when our story begins, the French were following their former American allies in the path of revolution. In their case the experiment got out of hand. Their king perished on the guillotine; the République became a military dictatorship; Europe was plunged into warfare that lasted with brief intermissions until 1815, when Napoleon was finally overthrown. America too was involved in the world conflict; and even when the fighting ended and Napoleon was consigned to fretful exile in the island jail of St. Helena, the unrest continued to spread, old empires to crumble. Spain lost most of her provinces in the New World; in the Old World Greece, Italy, and other areas were in turmoil.

In the United States, where that "first distinct, solemn assertion of the rights of men" had been made, the era had revealed an astonishing growth. Looking back from the vantage point of 1839, a writer in the *Democratic Review* claimed that his country had achieved half a century of "progress in all the substantial elements of national grandeur which is believed to have had scarce a parallel in the annals of mankind." The new science of statistics made good reading for Americans, for everything that could be measured had got bigger and better during the fifty years since the establishment of the Constitution in 1789. The territory of the Union, according to the *Democratic Review*, had increased threefold, "without conquest or violence." Population had quadrupled, from less than four million to about sixteen million. Exports had increased in roughly the same proportion, from an annual value of under $20 million to between $80 and $100 million in the closing years of the 1830's. The nation's shipping tonnage had tripled. National revenue had expanded so as to provide a comfortable surplus of "some twenty or thirty millions of dollars yearly, instead of only three or four millions, as at first." The national debt was entirely paid off by 1835.

The *Democratic Review* listed other achievements with the same justifiable gratification. "A respectable Army and Navy, as well as the Judiciary, Legislative, Executive and other establishments of the Government, have, during the same period, been organized and respectably maintained." Forts, navy yards, and dry docks had been constructed. In 1789 America's coastline was marked by only eight or ten lighthouses; in 1839 by two hundred and fifty. Harbors had been improved, rivers and lakes rendered more navigable, roads and public buildings constructed. From a mere seventy-five post offices, scattered about the Union, the number had soared to over twelve thousand. There were now twenty-five hundred miles of canals, though none had existed while Washington was in office; and the railroads "beginning only ten or twelve years ago, are already completed over one thousand miles" (the figure was actually almost three times as large). Schools, colleges, lyceums, and institutes were multiplying in scores.

To this glorious extent, said the patriotic journalist (paraphrasing the poet Milton), had the American commonwealth, "unterrified and free . . . spread its wings like a young eagle, opened its undazzled eye to the midday sun, and, soaring far aloft, purged and unsealed her long abused sight at the fountain itself of heavenly radiance; while the whole noise of timorous and flocking birds, with those also that love the twilight, flutter about, amazed at what she means, and in their envious gabble would prognosticate a year of sects and schisms."

A fine piece of spread-eagle prose. The facts, though, were incontrovertible whatever the interpretations put upon them—and whatever the less attractive sides of the story might be. America's first half-century of independence under the Union was in truth a time of extraordinary growth. When George Washington was inaugurated as first President of the United States at New York City in 1789, only eleven of the thirteen states had ratified the new constitution. It was not certain that the recalcitrant two, Rhode Island and North Carolina, would change their minds; Rhode Island, in the throes of "democracy," was particularly stubborn. Several others had ratified only after heated debates, and with the understanding that the Constitution would be amended as quickly as possible by the addition of a bill of rights. There was considerable dissension, in and out of Congress, but as yet there were no political groupings to regulate and focus conflict. There was an alarming national debt, and the individual states were likewise in financial straits. New York was a mere temporary home for the federal government; "Federal City," which was to be christened Washington, District of Columbia, did not even exist on an architect's drawing board; its very location was as yet unknown. The President was acutely conscious of the difficulties that lay ahead and of his own lack of training to deal with them.

What a contrast with the situation in 1837, when Martin Van Buren was inaugurated as America's eighth President! The Union now consisted of twenty-six states, the most recently admitted of which were Arkansas (1836) and Michigan (1837). Others, created from the territories between the Mississippi and the Rocky Mountains, would join them in due course. There was still considerable dissension in and out of Congress. Sectional controversy was casting a portentous shadow across the future: the day before Van Buren's inauguration, in March, President Jackson recognized the formal independence of the Republic of Texas, and later that year an Illinois mob at Alton murdered Elijah P. Lovejoy because he was an abolitionist. But there were full-fledged political parties to reconcile or at least represent the varied shades of local and sectional opinion within the vast country. The federal government was firmly ensconced in Washington, D.C., though the Capitol and other federal buildings were still under construction.

The look of the land had altered; so, profoundly, had the personnel. Such was the speed of change, such the compression of the American time scale, that the Founding Fathers were now remote, awesome, and shadowy figures. Of the previous presidents, Washington himself was long in his Mount Vernon grave; John Adams and Thomas Jefferson had died—with a symbolic symmetry rare in history and not lost upon their contemporaries—within a few hours of one another, at Quincy in Massachusetts and Monticello in Virginia, on July 4, 1826; James Madison had lingered on, in poverty and comparative obscurity, until 1836; James Monroe, likewise impoverished, had died five years earlier. Only John Quincy Adams—grim, combative "old man eloquent"—serving in the House of Representatives as a member from Massachusetts, and Andrew Jackson, who was about to retire to his western home in Tennessee, were surviving. Aaron Burr had hung on quietly until 1836, thirty-two years after the duel in which he killed Alexander Hamilton. John Jay had clung to life until 1829. Chief Justice John Marshall had remained a force in the land until 1835. But most of the other great men of the Revolutionary era and the early Republic—Sam Adams, Benjamin Franklin, John Hancock, Patrick Henry—had gone many years before.

True, there was a continuity in government, in fact a presidential tradition. Of the pre-Jacksonian figures, all except the two Adamses—father and son—were Virginians; after Washington all, including the Adamses, had stepped into the presidency from the vice-presidency or the secretaryship of state. With Andrew Jackson another atmosphere prevailed. Yet even he came out of the historic haze of revolutionary America, though he had been little more than a pugnacious boy at the time. With Martin Van Buren of New York the case was different. Fifteen years the junior of Jackson, a veteran in politics but not in war or constitution-making, he was the first American President to be born after the Declaration of Independence. No special aura of the past, he knew, surrounded him. He was a manipulator, the Sly Fox of Kinderhook. "Unlike all who have preceded me," Van Buren confessed in his inaugural speech of 1837, uneasy in grammar and apologetic in tone, "the Revolution that gave us existence as one people was achieved at the period of my birth; and whilst I contemplate with gratified reverence that memorable event, I feel that I belong to a later age and that I may not expect my countrymen to weigh my actions with the same kind and partial hand."

His countrymen had in actuality never shown marked kindness in commenting upon the actions of his predecessors. Still, Van Buren was remarking on an obvious truth when he emphasized the distance between himself and the others. Anyone who compared Van Buren with George Washington and John

"Half a Century of Progress"

Adams could see that the nation had traveled a long way. Van Buren with his quick, temporizing, managerial skill, his tact, and his professional affability, belonged to another world than that of Washington, the Virginia planter and soldier-hero, with his "immutable taciturnity," his handsome clothes, his crested coach, his retinue of white servants and black slaves, another world than that of peevish, learned, sober John Adams. The costume, demeanor, vocabulary, and acts of Washington and Adams linked them with the America of what might almost be called antiquity, just as Van Buren's costume and gestures and turns of phrase established him as a representative of the American Democracy.

Did the change amount to a second revolution? Was the shift in America as great from 1789 to 1837 as that in contemporary Britain—from the reign of George III to that of the young princess, Victoria, who came to the throne in the same year that Van Buren moved to the White House? Or as in France, where no small gulf separated the reign of Louis XVI from that of Louis Philippe? Was it even more dramatic than these?

Much, it is clear, had been initiated, developed, defined in the America of our period. The process as it could be recorded and gauged in treaties, maps, almanacs, treasury returns, and statistical tables is described in the four chapters that follow. Here are the external lineaments of young America, the story of progress that the *Democratic Review* and many another source chronicled with such pride. It is a straightforward saga that requires no further explanation at this stage. But the three final chapters, which examine deeper aspects of American experience, do perhaps call for an introductory word.

First, their organization. In analyzing the half-century, historians have frequently chopped it into short chronological

The Nation Takes Shape

blocks, each corresponding to a presidential administration or to a political alignment. Thus, we are accustomed to read of the "Federalist Era" of Washington and Adams, 1789–1801; of "Jeffersonian America," 1801–9; of "Madison and the War Years," 1809–17; of Monroe and the "Era of Good Feeling," 1817–25; of J. Q. Adams and the "Revival of Party Spirit," 1825–29; of "Jacksonian America," 1829–37. Useful, unexceptionable divisions.

But they have certain drawbacks. They focus too exclusively upon the federal government, as if the essential story were contained in the character of individual presidents and in the outcome of congressional debates. Much of the story is exemplified within the arena of national government and politics, but not the whole story. Again, conventional interpretative frameworks assign an arbitrary quality—"Good Feeling," "The Rise of Nationality," "Jacksonianism"—to brief periods of years, as if the quality were confined to those few years, and were sudden in genesis and abrupt in transition. Such interpretations push into the background the local, state, or regional situation, except insofar as this may be reflected in Congress. They are likely to oversimplify conflicts and to portray American history as though it were almost entirely a matter of conflicts. The harmonies, the continuities, or the sheer weight of popular indifference may be equally important.

This is not to say that the half-century should be viewed always as a whole, without chronological subdivisions. One could make a good argument for splitting it in half at the year 1815, a year in some respects more crucial for the United States than it was for Europe. The period 1789–1837 is not a perfect entity, any more than other equivalent spans of time. History is a continuum; we risk falsification by isolating a segment of it, as we must do for practical purposes.

But in this instance we are perhaps justified in attempting to assess the period as a whole, and to seek its broader characteristics in the three final chapters. There is nothing particularly novel in doing so. Much recent historiography has avoided, or at least qualified, the conventional chronological arrangement mentioned above. "Jacksonianism" and other movements have been subjected to detailed investigation. The results, while still indefinite, are full enough to permit a description of this vital era in fairly wide terms.

That it *was* vital, and that in many ways it is still bafflingly unknown to us, may emerge in the course of this book. After dealing with America's surface achievements during half a century, we must come to grips with its inner history and try to answer the questions that arise when one looks again at the *Democratic Review* and at Channing's oration. That American nationality, American democracy, the American temperament, as we recognize them today, existed in outline by 1837 should become evident in the course of this narrative. In 1789 a group of revolted colonies embarked upon their fateful experiment, under the tutelage of the man who had led them to victory by armed resistance. Forty years afterward a French observer, Alexis de Tocqueville, was able to theorize on what we may with a few reservations call a finished product, the American character. When and by what means did it finally evolve?

According to the *Democratic Review*, America owed its success to a rare combination of "position and principles. . . . We have started forward in a benign climate, with abundance of healthy food, with great exemptions from the waste of wars,

9

and perfect liberty in the choice of business and place of settlement," in a land almost as large as Europe. These circumstances are examined in chapters ii–iv; they refer to America's "position."

The "principles" are the theme of chapters vi–viii. Channing felt that the "one commanding characteristic" of the age was "the tendency in all its movements to expansion, to diffusion, to universality. . . . This tendency is directly opposed to the spirit of exclusiveness, restriction, narrowness, monopoly which has prevailed in past ages." Did he mean that the new tendency was not apparent until the age of Jackson and Van Buren? Did he signal a fresh movement or one that was coeval with American independence?

To what extent American attributes were already formed by 1789, how much they developed from something else, what these attributes were, and why they did not lead to disaster, despite dire predictions to the contrary—these are questions of infinite scope and significance. How much the "democratic bent" is a peculiarly American phenomenon, and how much part of a common Western heritage; what its inherent strengths and shortcomings are—these too are vast questions germane to the subject of this book, which is, in a word, the shaping of the American nation.

II

The Union Defined: Government, Politics, and Law

In the struggle for independence against Britain the need, in Benjamin Franklin's vivid phrase, was to make thirteen clocks strike as one. Such unanimity of effort was never achieved by the thirteen colonies. Nor did they contrive to act smoothly together under the Articles of Confederation. They would not have met to revise their form of federal government, nor would the resulting Constitution have been ratified by the necessary majority of individual state conventions, if there had not been a substantial measure of agreement that some reform, some more unifying element, was needed. As a Philadelphia journalist said in 1788, in another memorable phrase, "thirteen staves and ne'er a hoop will not make a barrel."

George Washington's task as America's first chief executive was, in conjunction with Congress and the federal judiciary, to provide the hoop. His great advantage lay in his unique popularity. He more than any other person or institution *was* the hoop. With the possible exception of the ailing and aged Franklin, he was the only American of truly national stature. The unanimous choice of the electoral college that had been established under the new Constitution to select the President, Washington was at the moment of his inauguration in April, 1789, just fifty-seven years of age, a man of immense dignity and prestige. For eight and a half years he had conducted the war against the mother country. Then, with what his admiring countrymen felt was a supreme modesty, he had retired from public life to attend to his Virginia estates. Drawn reluctantly back into the limelight, he had presided over the Constitutional Convention in 1787, and the knowledge that he was so intimately associated with the new instrument of government did much to reassure his hesitant compatriots that here was a respectable enterprise, worthy of support. It followed inevitably that he should be chosen as President—and, much less inevitably, that John Adams of Massachusetts, a distinguished spokesman for American liberty, should be elected as Vice-President to balance the appointment. Sectionally, Massachusetts (the North) canceled out Virginia (the South).

Apart from what he stood for in the eyes of Americans, Washington had solid qualifications for office. For many years a member of the Virginia colonial legislature, he was acquainted at first hand with parliamentary procedure. As commander-in-chief he had grown accustomed to administration on a large scale; his relations with state governors and with the Continental Congress had taught him a good deal, if largely of a cautionary nature: this, as he usually saw it, was how things should *not* be run. Honest, straightforward, prudent, admired, he believed in the possibilities of the Union even if he doubted his own capacities. He believed in a central government that should be capable of uniting the states, promoting peace and industry, and negotiating firmly with foreign powers.

These were his views, and these his talents for office. Certain things needed to be done, certain dangers to be avoided. Beyond that, as Washington uneasily confided to his associates, he was in the dark. Providence, he presumed in his inaugural address, was on the side of the United States; the young nation needed all the protection it could get, supernatural or otherwise.

Washington's own deficiencies for the task ahead were those of nearly all his fellow countrymen. Few, for instance, were experts on foreign affairs or on financial matters, and in those fields he himself was relatively unversed. But what he knew by instinct and experience was also known to a considerable number of Americans. Of the twenty-two senators who formed the upper house of the first Congress and the fifty-nine members of the House of Representatives, no less than fifty-four had had a hand in the making of the Constitution, as delegates either at the Philadelphia Convention or at state ratifying conventions or both. Some, like James Madison in the House of Representatives, had already made contributions of permanent importance. If the standard of intelligence and integrity was uneven, there was enough of both to justify some confidence in the progress of the Union.

There were also, it is true, enough signs of latent and open conflict to cause alarm. Individual states were jealous of their privileges, in some ways more self-consciously at odds than when they had all been British colonies. A Governor Hancock of Massachusetts, a Clinton of New York, or a Patrick Henry of Virginia stressed his authority with keener sensibility than his royal predecessor had done. Sectional differences and antipathies were strongly marked. If a South Carolina planter regarded a man from New England as a mean trader and a hypocrite in religion, the New Englander was apt to view the Southern planter as proud, ignorant, and indolent. More seriously, there was widespread suspicion of the new Constitution, as a document subject to misinterpretation that would place too much power in the hands of the national government, and especially within the hands of some clique that might seize the reins of government.

These strains within the Union will be analyzed later. It is sufficient now to note that—so various were the prejudices, the opinions, the interests involved—every step taken to define the Union met with opposition. The vehemence of dispute had many causes. Some were unworthy, some unnecessary. Some, however, are understandable because of the newness of the Union. In this era the blank page was being written on. Whatever was written would remain, as precedent, custom, law, either to blight or to bless posterity. No wonder that the President's hands shook as he held his inaugural address and read out its blameless sentiments.

The Constitution was only a halfway covenant. In places it was silent on a point of detail, or a policy to be taken, because the problem had not occurred to the Philadelphia delegates. In other places it was silent or deliberately vague, because the delegates preferred to gloss over a controversial problem.

Among other things, the Constitution did not cover every detail of the executive branch. On one topic where it was specific, the question of a "compensation" for the President, Washington attempted to controvert the clause by proposing that he serve without pay other than his expenses. Fortunately for himself and his successors, Congress proceeded to vote him a substantial annual salary—$25,000, enough to maintain a hand-some style. Many other, more crucial issues were left open. Thus, there was no provision for executive departments beyond the brief statement (Art. II, sec. 2) that the President "may require the Opinion, in writing, of the principal Officer in each of the executive Departments, upon any Subject relating to the Duties of their respective Offices." However, common sense and the pattern set up under the Articles of Confederation were a useful guide. Henry Knox, Washington's former artillery chief, a fat, jolly, energetic man of thirty-nine, was continued in office as head of the War Department. Samuel Osgood, who had been a member of the Treasury Board, was installed as Postmaster General. More significantly, the Treasury Board was consolidated and power intrusted to one man as Secretary of the Treasury. The man was Alexander Hamilton, a brilliant and vigorous soldier, lawyer, and political journalist who was still in his early thirties. A former aide-de-camp of Washington, Hamilton had been a prominent figure at the Philadelphia Convention and then at the New York ratifying convention. Part-author—together with Madison and John Jay—of the masterful *Federalist* papers, he was considered by the President a man of exceptional promise.

The other prime executive post Washington allotted to a fellow Virginian. Under the Confederation, the Department of Foreign Affairs was the responsibility of John Jay, a New York lawyer, aged forty-four, who had served his country in the peace negotiations with Britain and as a diplomatist in Spain. Redesignated now by Congress as the Department of State, with somewhat extended functions, it came under the supervision of Thomas Jefferson, who at the time was American minister to France and who therefore could not take office until several months after Hamilton and the others. Forty-six years old, drafter of the Declaration of Independence, former governor of Virginia, planter-savant and diplomatist, Jefferson was an obvious choice as Secretary of State. The small group of executive heads was completed by Edmund Randolph, also of Virginia, as Attorney General. During the whole of the period only one other executive branch, the Navy Department (1798), was to be created. Randolph's appointment resulted from the Judiciary Act of 1789, which also enlarged on the Constitution's provisions for a federal court system, providing at the head a Supreme Court consisting of a Chief Justice and five associates. For his first Chief Justice, Washington chose John Jay.

Congress also gave early attention to a bill of rights, the omission of which from the Constitution had occasioned loud complaint from suspicious citizens. Hamilton and others had pointed out in 1787–88 that several states—including New York, where he was met with particularly active opposition—had not troubled to incorporate a specific bill of rights within their own constitutions. Moreover, many individual rights were in fact safeguarded, if incidentally, by the federal Constitution. But such explanations were not thought satisfactory. There was a widespread demand for an enumeration, item by item, of the American's right to freedom of speech, freedom of worship, freedom of assembly, trial by jury, and so on. In Massachusetts and elsewhere, ratification of the Constitution had been secured with the tacit agreement that a bill of rights would subsequently be added to it. The House of Representatives therefore, in September, 1789, drew up twelve amendments, based on the stipulations of individual states. Following the procedure indicated in the Constitution (Art. V), these were submitted to the states for ratification by the necessary three-fourths majority. In the event, only ten amendments were ratified. They were appended to the Constitution, as the "Bill of Rights," at the end of 1791. Some of them have rarely been invoked since then. One or two, especially the Fifth Amendment, have covered more situations than were ever dreamed of in the philosophy of the Founding Fathers. The immediate effect was happy. Criticisms of the purport of the Constitution died down, and the amendments helped to appease North Carolina and Rhode Island and so bring them into the Union.

This much was fairly plain sailing. So was the drawing of lots by which (under Art. I, sec. 3) the senators divided themselves into three groups, their terms to expire respectively in two, four, and six years, in order to establish the future sequence in which one-third would retire every second year. Article I, section 6 ("The Senators and Representatives shall receive a Compensation for their Services") was also decided without undue delay, on the basis of a combined living and mileage allowance.

There was trouble in reaching agreement over "such District (not exceeding ten miles square) as may, by Cession of particular States, and the Acceptance of Congress, become the seat of the Government of the United States" (Art. I, sec. 8). Philadelphia was still the largest city in the Union, but it was being overtaken in population by New York. Both put forward their claims, New York as the host which had gone to some trouble to fit out Federal Hall, Philadelphia as the historic home of American independence and constitutional union. In the outcome, both were disappointed. A new site was chosen near Georgetown on the Potomac, only a few miles upriver from Washington's home at Mount Vernon. "Federal City," in a ten-mile square known as the District of Columbia, began to be surveyed and laid out in 1791 under the enthusiastic direction of a Frenchman, Pierre L'Enfant. As some solace to Philadelphia, the federal government moved there in December, 1790, in preparation for another and final move in 1800 to Federal City. When Congress began its deliberations in Philadelphia, the site of the future Capitol was still covered by a wood; and several years afterward the British poet Thomas Moore could still with some truth poke fun at Washington, D.C., in the presidency of Thomas Jefferson, as

> This embryo capital, where Fancy sees
> Squares in morasses, obelisks in trees;
> Which second-sighted seers, ev'n now, adorn
> With shrines unbuilt and heroes yet unborn.
> Where nought but woods and Jefferson they see,
> Where streets should run and sages *ought* to be.

Thus far, the President had not played an assertive part in the direction of affairs. Indeed, no one could precisely envisage his powers and duties. In some respects his office was ceremonial in character. The appropriate degree of ceremony was open to debate. By temperament Washington favored a certain formality, and his advisers recommended as much dignity as was compatible with American taste. The solutions that Washington arrived at were not uniformly welcomed. His official tours of the New England states in 1789 and of the southern states in 1791 were in general approved, though in this instance he set no precedent. Future presidents did not make a regular habit of personally investigating the conditions of the Union. But his pattern of weekly levees and small dinners was criticized by some as being too stiff; Washington had little small talk, and his overawed guests were sometimes frozen with embarrassment. Here again there was no decisive precedent; his successors, after John Adams, tended to show less formality in social intercourse. However, even in their case the office of President did imply a certain distance, a degree of protocol. Perhaps it was inevitable. At any rate, Washington did not make the mistake of undue affability: no one could accuse him of backstairs alliances.

The President was the ceremonial head of state. He was also the chief executive, in whom the Constitution vested various powers. His relations with Congress required definition beyond the general prescriptions of the written word. In some ways he interpreted his own authority modestly, for like most of his contemporaries he did not conceive of his office as the source of all directive energy. Most of the early legislation, with a few important exceptions, originated with Congress. The veto power granted him by the Constitution he exercised only twice, though that was sufficient to initiate the practice and encourage later presidents to be more free in its use.

It had been anticipated that the Senate, under the chairmanship of the Vice-President, would serve as the President's privy council and work in close collaboration with him, much as the governor's council had done in Washington's own colonial Virginia. Composed initially of less than thirty members, it was a compact body of influential men. Actually, the Senate and executive never grew close. If Washington could be accused of too much formality, so could Congress. An almost absurd amount of punctilio surrounded the deliberations of the early congresses. As might be expected of the senior and smaller body, the Senate was more clannish than the House. Its first sessions were held behind closed doors, with no reporting permitted.

The Nation Takes Shape

Washington's only attempt at close co-operation with the Senate in the formulation of foreign policy, in 1789, was therefore not surprisingly a failure. He arrived in person, to propose the form of a treaty that he wished to negotiate with the Creek Indians on the southern frontier. The Senate, touchy and unprepared, was unwilling to commit itself in his presence. He, according to Maclay of Pennsylvania—a somewhat hostile witness—showed a regrettable impatience and never repeated the experiment. Thereafter, presidents did not send treaties to the Senate for ratification until they had been drawn up and provisionally agreed upon between the executive and the foreign power concerned.

Washington showed a similar firmness in two other encounters in this debatable ground where the legislative and executive functions overlapped. By the Constitution he was obliged to submit the names of executive appointments to the Senate for advice and consent. But the initial choice lay with him, and he established the further, vital principle that the right of dismissal also lay with him. The second encounter took place in 1796, with the House of Representatives, when a majority refused to accept a treaty—Jay's Treaty, with Britain—that had already been ratified by the Senate. The House argued that it too must have a share in the formulation of foreign policy, since it controlled the purse strings of the federal government: no approval, no appropriation. Washington and his advisers took an unyielding stand, however, and the area of treaty-making remained the joint concern of executive and Senate, with the latter in a relatively passive role.

But who *were* Washington's advisers, if the Senate failed to develop into his privy council? At the outset he consulted whoever seemed best equipped to help him. The Chief Justice refused the role—quite properly, in view of the future role of the judiciary. James Madison, in the House, was more obliging. Washington sought his opinion on a variety of topics and even, when he contemplated retirement at the end of his first four-year term, got Madison to draft a farewell address. The President's other mainstay, in the groping early months, was Treasury Secretary Alexander Hamilton. Clear-witted, persuasive, ambitious, energetic, Hamilton labored to set the administration on what he felt to be the right lines. When Thomas Jefferson returned from Paris to become Secretary of State in March, 1790, he too was called upon for advice and responded with almost the same fluent readiness as Hamilton. The Vice-President, Secretary for War, Attorney General, and Postmaster General were consulted to a lesser extent. By the end of Washington's first term, quite unwittingly, he had gone a long way toward creating a "cabinet," though neither the word nor the notion had been mentioned in the Constitution. A good many years were to elapse before the institution was formally recognized or finally accepted.

Still, by the end of his second term Washington's "cabinet" was known and recognized by the name. Its composition was altered, not simply because all the original members had gone—Jefferson in December, 1793, Hamilton in January, 1795—but because Washington had replaced them by men whose views more or less coincided with his own. Hitherto, there had been no doctrine of executive unanimity. The President's main duty had been, it seemed to Washington, to preside, much as he had presided over the Constitutional Convention. He was not debarred from holding views of his own, but neither was he obliged to set the pace of legislation. That was a task in which the initiative lay principally with Congress and with the executive departments.

In this view he was sustained by the body of informed opinion. Jefferson, for instance, and some of his radical-minded friends feared that the President might usurp authority, that by some kind of law of governmental degeneration and concentration plain George Washington or one of his successors might turn before their eyes into an overweening George III. Jefferson did not like the loophole in the Constitution that made it possible for a President to be re-elected an indefinite number of times; in that direction lay hereditary despotism. Hamilton, on the other hand, who later summed up Washington as "an Aegis very essential to me," apparently visualized the President as a figure somewhat akin to a constitutional monarch—strictly limited, no doubt, in prerogatives—with himself as an American version of a prime minister.

The analogy proved to be false, though it was plausible for Hamilton to compare himself with the younger Pitt in the British Parliament. Pitt, another brilliantly precocious politico, was Chancellor of the Exchequer (and head of the treasury) as well as Prime Minister. Why should not Hamilton, who like many others in America and Europe genuinely admired the British mode of government, aspire to a similar position? American finances needed to be put in order; he was the executive head with the most urgent program to implement, with the sharpest ideas of what he meant to do, and with the boldest desire to shape the national government accordingly.

But Congress was not Parliament, and the President was not a monarch—pliant or despotic. Unlike Pitt, Hamilton and the other American "cabinet" members had and could have no seat in the legislature. Article I, section 6, prescribed that "no Person holding any Office under the United States, shall be a Member of either House during his Continuance in Office." The aim, as elsewhere in the Constitution, was to separate the branches of government. The effect was to isolate the branches from one another, to draw the executive heads into closer rapport with the President, and to present difficulties of co-operation that were by no means overcome by the presence in the Senate of the Vice-President, magistral but passive except for his casting vote in the event of deadlock. At first Hamilton endeavored to deal in person with the House. His efforts were unavailing. Congress decided in January, 1790, that henceforth the Treasury Secretary should submit reports in writing.

The ties gradually established between President and Congress were of an unlooked-for nature, for they were the ties of party politics. Not only did the Constitution make no reference to political parties; the Founding Fathers viewed the possibility with gloomy suspicion. Parties were the mark of Old World corruption, the resort of "placemen," the machinery of "influence." They were also the symptoms of disunion, the sign that the centrifugal tendencies of the loosely knit nation were triumphing over its centripetal aspects. How could the center hold, once discordant views became organized and institutionalized?

Intelligent Americans, James Madison among them, realized even before the Constitution went into effect that the Union was bound to embrace different and differing points of view. Indeed, the very contest of minority interests was the best guarantee of stability, or at least of justice; a majority could not tyrannize over the rest so long as society represented so many divisions of geography and sentiment. Washington also, before he became President, understood that there were various interests to be considered and that each had a right to be heard. He and his associates were disappointed but not horrified when the tussle over the Constitution in 1787–88 seemed to throw the land into opposing camps of Federalists and Antifederalists. As the *Massachusetts Centinel* commented at the end of 1788,

> Antis, and Feds, usurp the glory,
> So long enjoy'd by Whig and Tory.

Some disputation was only to be expected. The disquieting feature was that the uproar continued. It was not quite the same argument. Within a remarkably short time the Constitution was accepted, and almost enshrined, by Americans of every political stripe. They competed vigorously in protestations of fidelity to it. But the temple of American liberty became also the bull ring of American political controversy. And the strife was nowhere more bitter, in the first years of Washington's administrations, than within his own executive branch.

Trouble did not erupt immediately. In June, 1790, the President could write, "I feel myself supported by able coadjutors who harmonize extremely well together." But during the next five years his situation was considerably less rosy. While there was passionate concern to "form a more perfect Union" and to "promote the general Welfare," there was passionate disagreement as to the best means of accomplishing those wholesome ends. A sizable proportion of the House, and several senators, were ready to interpret the Philadelphia Convention as the opening gambit of a maneuver designed to weaken the states and place authority in the hands of "monocrats," aristocrats, speculators. The "wise and the good," on the other hand, felt that the Union still needed to be cemented more firmly against "mobocrats" and debtors.

Alexander Hamilton not only felt this; he was determined to take positive action. He believed what he said, but his techniques of persuasion lent color to his opponents' belief that he was an unscrupulous cynic. At least this was the interpretation given to his three impressively argued reports, *Public Credit* (January, 1790), *National Bank* (December, 1790), and *Manufactures* (December, 1791). His contentions were logical and coherent, the fruit of convictions held for several years. They were that union and prosperity must be synonymous; that the national government must be put on a sound financial footing; that it must honor its obligations (which were considerable, having been incurred in the Revolutionary War) and those of individual states incurred in the same cause; that it must fund a national debt, to be paid off by gradual stages; that the transaction would strengthen national loyalties by giving men a financial stake in federal securities; that there must be a national bank to lend additional stability to the economy; and that the federal government had both the right and the duty to levy taxes, to develop commerce, and to encourage manufactures.

He was able to carry out much of the program, with the slightly hesitant approval of the President and in face of anguished protest by the Secretary of State. A Bank of the United States—in actuality a private bank with national responsibilities, like the Bank of England—was chartered by Congress for a twenty-year period, in February, 1791, after two months of fierce debate. It was, one senator asserted, "an aristocratic engine"; and a generation later its successor, the second "B.U.S.," was to be assailed in much the same terms. When the first bank was chartered, Hamilton had already undergone a prolonged battle over the problem of America's debts. No one seriously contested his plan to pay off the sums owed to foreign creditors—to the French government and to Dutch banking houses. Nor, when funding was under discussion, did his opponents in Congress condemn the principle of honoring domestic federal indebtedness. American creditors had as much right as foreign ones to be repaid for their financial assistance to the United States.

The objection to funding centered on Hamilton's proposal to ignore the previous intricate history of these paper securities, and simply to supply the present owners of federal certificates with new bonds at par. This intention disturbed even close associates of Hamilton. It shocked and enraged James Madison. The original holders, he maintained, had in most instances sold their depreciated securities at a discount. He urged that some effort be made to discriminate between the original holders, whose patriotism had left them with empty pockets, and the later swarm of speculators, who had snapped up the securities in the hope of realizing a quick profit. Such charges against "the corrupt squadron of paper dealers" (in Jefferson's phrase) were not entirely unfounded. Though Hamilton himself had clean hands, some of his friends were involved in unsavory deals. Madison's "discrimination" scheme, while complicated, was probably workable and certainly equitable. He and his followers had good reason to be angered by Hamilton's cleverly engineered victory over them in Congress.

The assumption of state debts was even more unpopular, at least in Pennsylvania and in the southern states. Several of them had already begun to discharge their obligations; the New

England states, which owed larger sums, had not. Why permit the national government to penalize one area in order to benefit another? Why indorse Hamilton's deliberate and cynical effort to base the Union upon the loyalty of a minority of powerful beneficiaries? Was allegiance to depend on plunder? Even assuming the soundness of Hamilton's broad plan, why saddle the country with a debt of $80 million when this total—as was fairly generally acknowledged—could without injustice have been scaled down by $10 million?

Hamilton, never at a loss for an answer, admitted in private that he aimed to attach men to the Union by financial ties: what others were as binding? In public, he stressed the impracticability of his enemies' opinions, the need to act quickly to establish the nation's credit (at home and abroad), and the fact that President Washington stood behind him, sagacious and incorruptible.

Little by little, the executive was equated with "Federalism" and its critics with "Republicanism." Both words, incidentally, had a checkered etymology. To the annoyance of the Republicans, their foes had stolen from them a designation, "Federalism," which in the first place stood for decentralization and state supremacy. Since the Federalists advocated the opposite, the voters of 1787–88 were somewhat confused. However, to the annoyance of the Federalists, their enemies had stolen from *them* a designation, "Republicanism," which applied to supporters of the Constitution and which therefore soon became a word in good patriotic standing. The voters were still more confused. In an effort to fasten another title, then in ill repute, upon their adversaries, the Federalists dubbed the followers of Jefferson "Democrats." The new-style "Republicans," with a dexterity since typical in American politics, accepted the challenge and incorporated the pejorative word in their title. They owned themselves to be "Democratic-Republicans."

Historians disagree in dating the birth of party politics in the United States. It is meaningless to search for any particular date. The "Feds" and "Antis" of 1788 are obviously in some ways the originators of the system. But there is not an uninterrupted line of descent from them to the Federalists and Republicans of a decade later, still less to the Whigs and Democrats of Martin Van Buren's era. Nor are we quite justified in dividing Americans of the 1790's into "Hamiltonians" and "Jeffersonians," though each man was in some degree the leader and exponent of a political cause. For one thing, not all Federalists were fervent admirers of Hamilton; he and John Adams, for instance, were far from friendly—Adams once spoke of his "damnable malice"—and their antipathy had important consequences in weakening the party. Not all Federalists were men of property; the back-country farmers of New England had little in common with "paper dealers" and voted for Federalism mainly because of admiration for the Constitution, or out of sectional pride. Again, Jefferson was reluctant to embroil himself in open controversy. His temperament was far less combative than Hamilton's. The overt attack upon Hamiltonian doctrine was headed by James Madison, who after collaborating with Hamilton in the *Federalist* papers had had misgivings and had become an ardent Virginian state-rights advocate; by the aggressive Virginia orator William Branch Giles; and by the Swiss-born Albert Gallatin of Pennsylvania, a young man of brilliant intellect with an ideologue's enthusiasm for the principles of Republicanism.

The Union Defined

However, before Washington's first administration was over there was vigorous opposition to the Hamiltonian programs he had indorsed. Washington himself was not yet the target of criticism, though Hamilton's opponents complained that the wily Treasury Secretary took shelter behind the prestige of the President. In 1790 the radical Senator Maclay of Pennsylvania felt strongly enough to write in his diary: "Would to God . . . General Washington were in heaven! We would not then have him brought forward as the constant cover to every unconstitutional and irrepublican act." By this time Hamilton, on his side, was equally ready to identify a malignant opposition. "Mr. Madison," he told a friend, "co-operating with Mr. Jefferson, is at the head of a faction decidedly hostile to me and my administration; and actuated by views . . . subversive of the principles of good government and dangerous to the Union, peace, and happiness of the country."

"My administration" is a revealing expression. In conjunction with some of Hamilton's other phrases, it suggests that he did in fact conceive of himself as the shaper of policy, and of Washington as a somewhat aloof guardian of the American character. Hamilton's precise motives are veiled from us, but there is no doubt that Washington for his part was acutely disturbed by the squabble within his own cabinet and by the cleavage in public sentiment. With good reason he was still more disturbed in 1793, when revolutionary France, having sent its king to the guillotine, declared war on Britain and most of Europe. Faction acquired a new bitterness in America, as the Federalists became identified with Britain ("Anglomen" in the Republican terminology) and the Republicans with France ("Gallomen" or "Jacobins").

The Nation Takes Shape

Washington had hoped to retire from the presidency in 1793. Now, with the country in ferment, begged by both Hamilton and Jefferson to remain, he had no alternative but to put away his intended farewell address and allow himself to be chosen a second time by the presidential electors. In doing so, and in insisting on retirement in 1797, he established a two-term tradition that was to persist until 1940—and to be grafted onto the Constitution by the Twenty-second Amendment in 1951. Not that every subsequent President succeeded in winning a second term—John Adams and John Quincy Adams had only one term each—but this became the typical pattern, followed by Jefferson, Madison, Monroe, and Jackson, and the pattern was broken—as with the two Adamses—only when the country was in the throes of some exceptional crisis or in the process of regrouping its major political allegiances.

Another consequence of faction was that Washington gradually changed his cabinet until all his executive heads were Federalist in outlook. It was not a very clear-cut policy at first —executive posts were not thought alluring in the 1790's, and Washington sometimes had to offer an appointment to several men before he found one who would accept. Later presidents did not experience this difficulty but were able to pick their appointees with a fairly accurate foreknowledge of the candidates' administrative capacity and political leanings. Party affiliation was to become an indispensable test of fitness for office.

Washington did not admit that he was evolving into a party chieftain. The admission might be discovered unwittingly in some observations in the last years of his life, when he described himself as a Federalist and referred to Republicans as a band of villains. The distinction is that he still resisted the idea of parties. Federalists, he felt, were men of sense and patriotism in the main. Republicans, with few exceptions, were fools and knaves, not *the* opposition but "opposition" in the sense of obstruction, misconduct, disloyalty. His immediate successor, John Adams, bedeviled by factional attitudes to foreign policy, was a shrewd man. Yet Adams too was reluctant to acknowledge that America had produced a two-party system. His reluctance was understandable, for the system was still in embryo and the lines of party warfare were distorted by personal and sectional rivalries. Washington's revised Farewell Address of 1796, which Hamilton had assisted in preparing, was regarded by some as a Federalist document, but its condemnation of party strife met with general approval. Jefferson, the Republican candidate in the presidential election of that year, was genuinely sorry that his friends had chosen him. On the Federalist side, Adams was genuinely pleased to stand as the Federalist candidate. But some Federalists, possibly encouraged by Hamilton, hoped that their vice-presidential candidate, Thomas Pinckney of South Carolina, would get more votes than Adams and so step into the presidency. Adams, it chanced, won the day by a narrow margin; he secured 71 electoral votes, Jefferson got 68, and Pinckney 59.

In short, party organization hardly existed, if by that we mean a coherent, disciplined apparatus, linking local and state groups in a nationwide chain. But the situation was rapidly changing, in part by accident and in part by design. The awkwardness of the electoral rule by which the two candidates with the highest separate votes became President and Vice-President was only too apparent when Federalist Adams found himself with Republican Jefferson for a partner. Even worse

31

was the dilemma in 1800, when Adams again confronted Jefferson. This time Jefferson beat him but tied in electoral votes with his Republican running mate, Aaron Burr. The tie threw the final decision, as the Constitution provided, into the House of Representatives. Thirty-six ballots and much unseemly wrangling were necessary to break the deadlock. Jefferson was installed as President, Burr consoled with the vice-presidency. There was every likelihood that similar clumsy crises would recur unless the defective electoral mechanism were improved. By the Twelfth Amendment, ratified in 1804, the procedure was therefore changed to insure that candidates for each office should be listed and voted for separately. Henceforward the two offices would in theory be occupied by men of compatible views, in fact of the same party. The Twelfth Amendment recognized within the Constitution that partisanship existed.

Henceforward, too, the vice-presidency would gradually decline in importance. During the half-century no President died in office, and after Jefferson only Van Buren would step into the White House from the vice-presidency. With Jefferson, one other minor precedent was established. Washington and Adams delivered their annual addresses on the state of the Union before Congress in person. Jefferson, recognizing the actuality of separation between executive and legislature, contented himself with annual messages in writing—a device to be followed by presidents for over a hundred years, until Woodrow Wilson reverted to the original method.

The outlines of national government and politics—and their equivalent patterns within each state—hardened. Executive and legislature took on living flesh to clothe the bones of the Constitution. In the thought of the Founding Fathers, federal re-

The Union Defined

publicanism was tripartite, not merely dual. The separation of powers, the checks and balances on which they and their commentators expended so much breath and ink, was not complete until the third side of the triangle was fitted in. Executive, legislative—and judiciary. There must be national courts and federal justices to bring the laws of the individual states into harmony with one another and, still more essential, with the higher law of the land as embodied in the Constitution. The executive and the legislature would enact further laws; the judiciary might insure that what they proposed was sanctioned by the Constitution.

On this general theory there was a measure of agreement. The first appeal in all disputes was to the text of the Constitution. Thus, when Hamilton and Jefferson were at loggerheads in 1791 over the proposal to charter a national bank and submitted their views to Washington, both took pains to show that the bank would or would not be constitutional, quite apart from the question of whether it would be desirable. Perhaps desirability was the real question. Neither Hamilton nor Jefferson had much difficulty in interpreting the Constitution to support his own case—Hamilton as a "loose constructionist" who maintained that there were implied powers in the document, Jefferson as the forerunner of many a "strict constructionist" who insisted that the Constitution meant what it said and nothing more. Still, this was the highest law, and there was evident need for a cool, learned, impartial interpretation of its Delphic clauses. The judiciary was, in Washington's words, "the chief pillar upon which our national government must rest."

For a while the Supreme Court remained relatively inactive.

33

The Nation Takes Shape

One of its six justices, John Rutledge of South Carolina, resigned after two years without having attended a single court session. Washington did not always find it easy to fill vacant seats. There were few early cases to decide, and the justices were kept excessively busy for a while with circuit duties. These duties required them—until the system was reformed—to hear cases wherever they came up. In *Chisholm* v. *Georgia* (1793) the court, arguing that the states had surrendered their sovereignty and could therefore be sued by individuals like any other body subject to the law of the land, was challenged by a massive weight of opinion. Its theory was squashed by the passage of the Eleventh Amendment (ratified in 1798), which declares in effect that a state may not be sued by a citizen of another state. In other respects also the court moved timidly and uncertainly.

Yet by degrees a powerful creed of judicial authority was being shaped. In the light of subsequent events, the court's initial prudences were to be a case of *reculer pour mieux sauter:* drawing back in order to make a bigger leap. Apparently showing the greatest circumspection in claiming jurisdiction, the court was half-consciously fashioning a new concept of judicial independence. America was to have, in the phrase popularized by the Massachusetts state constitution of 1780, "a government of laws and not of men." The federal justices began to define this government in ways not altogether envisaged by the Founding Fathers.

As they did so, their own authority imperceptibly increased, together with that of the federal over the state governments. *Ware* v. *Hylton* (1796) contended that federal treaties are paramount over state laws. In *Hylton* v. *U.S.* (1796), by upholding a federal tax, the court implied its function to decide the constitutionality of acts of Congress. Not until the appointment of John Marshall as Chief Justice, however, did the Supreme Court put on its full majesty. Marshall, a staunch Federalist from Virginia, had been acting briefly as John Adams' Secretary of State. As one of his last presidential acts, Adams imposed Marshall upon the Republican administration of Jefferson that followed his, in 1801. For a little spell Marshall acted cautiously, feeling his way into the judicial atmosphere. The first clash of his court with Thomas Jefferson, *Marbury* v. *Madison* (1803), was peculiarly negative in flavor; Marshall appeared to be limiting the jurisdiction of the court; yet in doing so he ruled that a section of the Judiciary Act of 1789 was unconstitutional and therefore void. The Supreme Court was not again to cancel the work of Congress in this manner until the Dred Scott decision of 1857. Nevertheless, the assertion of right, though rarely exercised, had been made.

In a long series of later decisions Marshall seems to have hypnotized his associates. The Federalist party of which he had been a member went down to defeat. The Republicans, once denounced as seditious intriguers, took over the federal government. The judicial appointments of Jefferson, Madison, and Monroe were made in favor of men thought to be Republicans. In vain: the Supreme Court continued as the stronghold of Federalist doctrine. The authority of the court itself, the authority of the national government over state governments, the sanctity of contracts (as in *Fletcher* v. *Peck*, 1810, and *Dartmouth College* v. *Woodward*, 1819), the implied power of Congress to legislate for the general welfare: all these "Hamiltonian" theorems were forcefully expounded by the extraordinary

John Marshall. "Let the end be legitimate," he insisted in *McCulloch* v. *Maryland* (1819), "let it be within the scope of the constitution, and all means which are appropriate, which are plainly adapted to that end, which are not prohibited, but consist with the letter and spirit of the constitution, are constitutional." Such views, though contrary to everything that Republicanism was supposed to stand for, usually gained a court majority. Was it the insidious magnetism of Marshall or some curious inherent tendency of the court itself that infected those who sat in its solemn garb to render judgment? Not until 1837, when John Marshall had at last died and yielded his place to Chief Justice Roger B. Taney, an appointee of Andrew Jackson, did the Supreme Court begin to take another tack. Even then it was to be characterized by a lofty conservatism. The tone, if not necessarily the political coloration, had been set by Marshall. For example, the rule of a majority decision, even if the majority were only of one, was accepted; dissenting opinions could be voiced, but they did not alter the court's simple vote. And the doctrines set forth in *Martin* v. *Hunter's Lessee* (1816), *Sturges* v. *Crowninshield* (1819), *Cohens* v. *Virginia* (1821), *Gibbons* v. *Ogden* (1824), and a score of other decisions steered the nation in a direction that was not easily reversible.

In fact by 1837, when Taney ruled in the Charles River Bridge case, the governmental, political, and legal lineaments of the Union were taking on permanent shape. Much was still in flux, especially in the vexed issue of federal in relation to state sovereignty, where despite Marshall's Supreme Court there was still extremely vigorous sentiment in favor of the states. The political system had undergone many changes and was to undergo many more.

The Union Defined

But the essentials were there. There had been and would be a great deal of controversy; yet the rules for skirmishing were understood, the zones of disagreement mapped. Most of the expedients available to the three branches of government had been tried out. As Justice William Johnson of South Carolina observed in *Anderson* v. *Dunn* (1824): "The science of government . . . practically consists in little more than the exercise of a sound discretion applied to the exigencies of the state as they arise. It is the science of experiment."

Thus, the right of impeachment guaranteed to the Senate in the Constitution had been tried out twice, both as a party maneuver and as an expression of hostility to the judiciary. The victims were two Federalist justices, John Pickering—a federal district judge in New Hampshire—and Samuel Chase of the Supreme Court. Though Pickering was found guilty and removed from office for unfitness, the case against Chase could not be sustained and the whole effort was something of a fiasco. Here, clearly, was an ineffectual procedure—"a mere scarecrow," Jefferson called it.

By 1837 the executive presented the spectacle of a President and cabinet that constituted a political team, linked more or less closely with their supporters in Congress. Where a majority in one or both houses of Congress was in opposition to the President, a situation of near-stalemate could arise, though the administration—unlike that in Britain—could not be displaced until its term was up. For this and many other reasons the presidency was a thankless office. Nevertheless it was a desperately sought-after office. The presidential bug bit almost every American political figure of any stature in the period. The torment of ambition is something to be reckoned with in the ca-

37

reers of William H. Crawford, Henry Clay, John C. Calhoun, and many another thwarted leader, not to mention the few aspirants who were successful.

As for the legislature, the Senate had developed into a distinguished and somewhat exclusive club. Its membership had increased to 52 as new states joined the Union, and its debates had ceased since 1794 to be held in private, but the Senate was still privileged in all sorts of ways and proud of its privileges. The House, with a two-year tenure of offce, had less coherence or prestige. But the House too, despite the discontinuity of membership, had its pride, traditions, big men. And what was lacking in intimacy was made up in size. By successive reapportionments of representation, its numbers grew from 59 in 1789 to 261 (including three delegates from Florida, Iowa, and Wisconsin Territories) in 1837.

Throughout the government, partisan politics had its influence (whether avowed or not). Politics was, it seemed to eyewitnesses, a national fever, endemic and perhaps chronic. There was always an election of some kind in the making. Issues were an intricate tangle of different types of bargain, feud, invocation. "It is impossible," Joseph Story of Massachusetts wrote from Washington in 1809, as a fledgling congressman, "for any man, who is not a representative, to appreciate the difficulties he has to encounter, in almost any subject of legislation in Congress. So many ingenious objections, and so many conflicting interests arise, that one is almost ready to decline the support of any proposition. I can very sincerely declare, that I would not continue in the public councils for a salary of $10,000 per annum."

Story was exceptional. Most Americans who entered politics

had a keen relish for the game. It had something for everybody, in the most material and in the most exalted sense. The profoundest problems of government, human nature, and posterity were at issue. So, at the other extreme, were the nicest manipulations for power and pelf. There were humbug and jobbery; there was also piety—the rich emotion stirred by Fourth of July orators when they alluded to the Declaration of Independence or to the Constitution. Thomas Jefferson once wrote of the Articles of Confederation, when they had been in operation for only six years, as "the good, old venerable fabric." It is a remarkable example of attachment to an instrument of government, in this case a rather ineffectual instrument. When the Constitution had been in operation for a similar period, though, commentators referred to it in the same sort of vocabulary, even though it served as a battleground of rival interpretations.

The conduct of national affairs was a subject of mingled ridicule, wonderment, praise, and blame in the eyes of foreigners who came to see for themselves what was going on in the baby-giant called the United States. We shall look now at that outside world, the Europe from which the travelers came, and at what had been done in the first half-century of independence to determine America's place among the nations.

III

The World Outside: Foreign Policy

In 1789 and immediately afterward, the countries of Europe were too engrossed in the affairs of their own continent to devote more than secondary attention to the United States. The great nations, in population, wealth, commerce, and military prowess, were France and Britain. Spain had declined, but she too was reckoned as a major power, still the mistress of a vast overseas empire. Russia, though a remote enigma, was a significant factor in world diplomacy. So were Austria and Prussia. In between these and the mass of petty principalities there were other states—Portugal, Denmark, the Netherlands—that were by no means negligible.

This is not to say that Europeans were unaware of the rest of the world, but that they were accustomed to think of it as an extension of Europe and Europe's problems. A sea fight in the Indian Ocean or the Caribbean, or a clash between mixed forces of whites and Indians in the forest wilderness of North America, was still in essence a European encounter.

The World Outside

How did the United States fit into the scheme? To both Britain and France, America represented a group of former colonies. True, these colonies had secured their independence, thanks to French aid. But their revolutionary war had been only part of a larger conflict between Great Britain and most of the rest of Europe. Britain had lost on the American mainland yet won nearly everywhere else. She consoled herself for the defection of the thirteen colonies by reflecting that she still retained enormous territories to the north, in what had been French Canada, as well as valuable possessions in the West Indies; that the thirteen colonies were a good riddance; that they would come to a bad end in their lawless, disunited, republican way; and that in any case their cultural and economic ties were still mainly with the mother country, so that American independence would be largely an illusion. Thus, the merchant shipping of Europe, for reasons that now seem incomprehensible, paid regular blackmail to the pirate nests of North Africa. American vessels in the Mediterranean formerly had been "protected" under these arrangements, as being within the British Empire. Now they had to pay their own way; and, failing to do so, they were suffering severely at the hands of Algerian pirates.

There was of course an element of pique in the British attitude to the United States—though some Englishmen were well disposed. Defeat had been humiliating; disdain and dislike were bound to follow. The new nation had never paid the debts to Britain recognized in the peace treaty of 1783. In turn the British had not settled American claims for compensation for slaves carried off during the Revolution. Moreover, the British, maintaining close connections with the Indian tribes of the back country and keenly interested in the profitable fur trade of the region, had ignored their treaty obligation to withdraw from the forts on American territory at Michilimackinac, Detroit, and elsewhere. The British commander at Fort Niagara even refused to allow American visitors to view the famous falls, and as late as 1794 the British established a further fortified trading post at the Maumee rapids, sixty miles into American territory from Detroit. Though the United States had her diplomatic representatives abroad (mere ministers, of inferior status to ambassadors), Britain did not trouble to send a properly accredited minister to the United States until 1791.

As for France, here too a certain coolness was observable. In the years from 1783 to 1789 the French had misgivings at the republican specter they had raised up in the New World. Nor, when all the mutual congratulations and some treaty recriminations died down after 1783, could the French forget that the war had cost them much in treasure, that the United States owed them a sizable sum, and that their own flag had until recently flown over much of North America. Thomas Jefferson, American minister to France in 1785–89, was unpleasantly conscious of the equivocal status of the United States, treated in the French court with strained politeness, as if it were a distant relative of doubtful morality. "We are," he said, "the lowest and most obscure of the whole diplomatic tribe." After the French Revolution broke out in 1789, the Franco-American link became emotionally stronger; ideologically, the infant nation could be regarded as father to the ancient one.

In Spain there was no such transformation. Monarchist Spain would give no encouragement to republicanism, especially since her own American colonies might emulate the example of the United States. Worse, the United States was contiguous with the Spanish Floridas and with Spanish Louisiana. Who could guarantee their survival—not to mention that of Cuba, Mexico, or the other Spanish possessions that stretched in a thinly held arc beyond the frontiers of the United States, all the way from Oregon and California to the Caribbean and the Orinoco? It was bad enough to confront the British in North America, still less agreeable to have to deal with the aggressive backwoodsmen of an aggressive new people. Spain had closed the Mississippi to American navigation; as American settlements continued to increase, far upriver in the Ohio Valley, she rightly feared for the future.

America, then, appeared to European diplomatists in 1789 as an awkward but junior interloper. None wholeheartedly wished her well; each had special grounds for hoping that the United States would run into difficulties.

The American reaction to Europe was bound up with her feeling about the nature and prospects of the Union. There was considerable distrust of Britain, heightened by British intrigues —real or imagined—in the frontier regions. There was growing indignation among westerners at what they interpreted as Spanish intransigence. There was a strong if inchoate belief that the United States was a special case among the nations of the world: the first popular republic, the first independent state in the American hemisphere, the first collection of European colonies to repudiate old allegiances. There was also widespread sympathy for France in the early years of its revolution.

These were only attitudes, not statements of policy. A statement was not called for until 1793; yet the controversy it initiated was to offer lengthy and heated proof that the United States was a vulnerable union, still feeling her way amid what Washington in his Farewell Address of 1796 was to call "our mutual cares, labors, and dangers." The problem was acute in the spring of 1793. Republican France, invaded by enemies, ousted them in a tremendous accession of nationalist energy and then proceeded to declare war upon Britain, Austria, Prussia, Sardinia, and the Netherlands. The President, after consulting his advisers, issued a proclamation of neutrality, and America was able to adhere to the policy embodied in it for nearly twenty years.

Yet not without anguish, dissension, and crises in which her neutrality seemed only nominal. What Washington no doubt had in mind, though he did not give it full expression until his Farewell Address, was a double necessity. America needed time and tranquillity in which to define herself; the mold of nationhood would not set if jostled. And she needed to stand aloof because she was *different* from Europe.

The double necessity was attended by a double difficulty. Neutral or not, she was split into rival parties by the European conflict. The struggle in the Old World, it could be maintained, aroused her more than any subsequent European war has done —at least in the initial stages. It did so because the conflict had many ideological overtones and because Americans had no clear, unified picture of their national interests in the field of foreign policy.

What Washington was to insist in the memorable language of 1796 might already be true, in theory, in 1793:

The great rule of conduct for us in regard to foreign relations is, in extending our commercial relations to have with them as little *political* connection as possible.

Europe has a set of primary interests which to us have none or a very remote relation. Hence she must be engaged in frequent controversies, the causes of which are essentially foreign to our concerns. Hence, therefore, it must be unwise . . . to implicate ourselves . . . in the ordinary vicissitudes of her politics. . . .

The World Outside

But Europe did not view America in this obliging light, and America, by the mere fact of her commercial relations, was bound to be implicated. The role of a neutral, as she was to discover after 1793 and again on later occasions, is a painful one. Popular with neither side, the neutral is likely to be roughly handled unless strong enough to resist, and few are strong enough when major powers become locked in a contest in which all but the overriding issues of the battle are thrust aside.

At home in America, the European war sharpened the party struggle. The Federalists, sickened by the excesses of the French Revolution, maintained that the world had gone mad. Sanity resided in Britain, where constitutional government, that most precious heritage, was still intact. The Republicans, reluctant like so many men in that amazing, sanguine, sanguinary era to admit that the principle of revolution was tainted, rallied to the side of France. After all, Jefferson urged and Washington's proclamation did not deny, the United States and France were still allies, bound to one another by the Treaty of 1778. France had sustained liberty in America; how in honor could America refuse aid to France when the scene was transferred to Europe? As Hugh Henry Brackenridge of Pennsylvania insisted in an open letter to the President in May, 1793, "The cause of France is the cause of man, and neutrality is desertion."

The war in Europe took on a character of near-deadlock. Gradually it became evident that France was master of the Continent and Britain of the high seas: "the tiger and the shark." Neither could vanquish the other, though Britain's Continental allies were conquered in spite of British subsidies and other encouragements.

Here America *was* important. To the French, the young United States appeared as a useful satellite nation whose nominal neutrality would be of greater benefit than her active participation as an ally. Misled by the enthusiasm that greeted his arrival at Charleston in 1793, the French republican minister Genêt concluded that he could achieve spectacular results in America. He could make the country an outpost of French revolutionary sentiment and also of recrudescent French imperialism. His aims were not so wild as some historians have argued. But his tactics were at fault. He behaved so outrageously—attempting to appeal to the American people over the heads of their government—that even ardent Republicans were disgusted by his antics. Genêt's successors, Fauchet and Adet, were not much more discreet in the next few years, intervening almost openly in America's domestic affairs. The interesting feature is that they failed, and they did so, as one of the more astute French observers realized in 1797, because:

Our agents wished to see only two political parties in the United States, the French party and the English party; but there is a middle party, much larger, composed of the most estimable men of the two other parties. This party, whose existence we have not even suspected, is the American party which loves its country above all and for whom preferences either for France or England are only accessory and often passing affections.

To the British, dismayed by the unfavorable trend of the war, America appeared in a different guise. Anglo-American friction was so serious by 1794 that open hostilities seemed probable. In addition to the grievances already mentioned, there was a minor disagreement over the exact line of the northeastern boundary with Canada, along the St. Croix River, and a series of more fundamental disputes over America's rights as a trading neutral. However, Washington on his part and the British cabinet on theirs were judicious enough to recognize the dangers in the situation. Washington sent Chief Justice John Jay to London in an effort to settle the principal difficulties between the two countries. Jay conferred amicably with the British Foreign Secretary, Lord Grenville, and by November, 1794, the two negotiators had compiled and signed the document familiarly described as Jay's Treaty.

When its contents became known in the United States early the next year, there was an instant outcry. Even Washington was disappointed. The Senate was barely persuaded, by a vote of 20 to 10, to ratify the treaty by the required two-thirds majority. Republicans assailed Jay as a traitor, a disguised Englishman who had tamely submitted to British pressure. Federalist defenders of the document—one of whom remarked that it had more critics than readers—were hooted down when they showed themselves on public platforms to explain its provisions.

In truth, the treaty was not a spectacular victory for American diplomacy. Jay did win the British promise to evacuate the frontier posts and to open parts of the empire—notably India and (with severe restrictions) the West Indies—to American shipping. Lord Grenville consented to the appointment of joint commissions which would attempt to resolve the Canadian boundary question, the matter of debts to Britain outstanding since before the Revolutionary War, and the American counterclaim for compensation in respect of British maritime confiscations. But nothing was said about compensation for slaves carried off in the Revolutionary War; the West Indies clause was, most Americans thought, a deprivation rather than a concession; and Grenville blandly refused to commit himself on the main issue of American maritime rights.

On Jay's side, it must be said that he got about as much as Britain was prepared to concede at that period. He could have pushed his case a little harder without wrecking the discussions, but he was hampered, though he did not realize it, by British secret information (gained in part through Hamilton's conversations with the British minister in Philadelphia) of America's weaknesses. Armed with this knowledge, Grenville felt safe in evading major controversies. There is no tenderness in international diplomacy. Jay on the whole did his best, and he was treated with reasonable candor and courtesy. His country's newness, her isolation, her neutrality, created grave problems for the United States. The signing of Jay's Treaty and its ratification (however grudging) by the Senate provided the first evidence that these same disadvantages might be sources of strength. Also, time was on her side. Five, ten, twenty years hence America would be a formidable adversary. Better, then, to defer a settlement where possible, since she would at some later stage be able to insist on a better bargain.

The maintenance of neutrality was not an easy task for George Washington or John Adams. Every step they took won them additional enemies in America. Thus, Washington was bitterly abused by Republicans for having sent a Republican envoy —James Monroe of Virginia—to France (at about the same time that Jay was dispatched to London) and then recalling him in 1796, furious and humiliated, on the grounds that Monroe had misrepresented Jay's Treaty in particular and the policy of his government in general. The French professed to regard the treaty as a hostile act, doubly hurtful in that the United States was still bound to them by the alliance of 1778. Franco-American relations deteriorated alarmingly. Monroe's successor, Charles C. Pinckney, was cold-shouldered when he arrived in Paris. When John Marshall and Elbridge Gerry joined him in October, 1797, to form a trio of commissioners, they did their best to negotiate a new treaty of friendship. But the French continued to display a mixture of contempt and irritation— these nicely blended in the demand by the three French commissioners for an official American loan to France and an unofficial bribe for Foreign Minister Talleyrand.

The Americans refused; the negotiations were broken off; and when Adams disclosed what the three Frenchmen (Messrs. "X, Y, Z") had been up to, Congress and the country at large responded with a burst of Francophobia as violent as the Francophilia of five years before. In 1793 Washington had been impelled toward war on the French side. In 1798 Adams was swept toward war against the French. Indeed for a while there was a kind of undeclared war; single American and French warships fought one another on several occasions, and a total of eighty-five French armed vessels were captured as prizes by America's small, hastily equipped navy. But Adams was cooler than his party. While prominent Federalists were urging a formal declaration of war, the President appointed another commission to France in 1799. His action was abused as gross cowardice, though it required great courage to incur the charge of appeasement when he could easily have permitted himself to be borne along on a wave of patriotic excitement.

Adams' conduct cost him his presidential career. Only in less heated retrospect were his countrymen able to see that he had acted in America's best interests; that, like John Jay, in this frail, formative era he had few good cards in his hand; and that the convention of 1800 signed by his three new commissioners did include French assent to America's withdrawal from the 1778 alliance. The alliance had not counted for much in the past few years, but its abrogation was a decisive gesture to Americans. Henceforth, in the celebrated words of Jefferson's first inaugural address (March, 1801), "peace, commerce, and honest friendship with all nations, entangling alliances with none," would stand as one of the "bright constellations" of guiding principles for the Republic.

The advantages of intelligent neutrality, meanwhile, were steadily more apparent. Thomas Pinckney, who in 1795 worked out the treaty that bears his name, scored a notable success in Spain. The Spanish now agreed to recognize the southern and western boundaries of the United States, which had been established in the Anglo-American peace treaty of 1783 but which had not yet gained international sanction. These frontiers were the thirty-first parallel of latitude to the south and the Mississippi to the west. Further, Pinckney secured the vital right to free navigation of that river, and to warehousing privileges in New Orleans or some other estuary port.

If Pinckney's Treaty seemed to promise more equitable dealings with Spain, Jay's Treaty introduced a genuine improvement in America's relationship with Britain. According to one capable historian, the years from 1795 to 1805—usually described as a decade of continuing Anglo-American friction—in fact marked a distinct rapprochement. The British withdrew from the western forts, as pledged, in 1796. Moderately successful arbitrations were carried out. Anglo-American commerce thrived. American ships were to be seen in every British-held port around the globe. The United States was Britain's best customer, and the British Empire likewise imported the bulk of what the United States had to offer. Moreover, the

The World Outside

British restrictions on neutral trade in wartime were leniently interpreted. So was the British system of naval impressment. Some American sailors were unjustly seized and held to service under the Union Jack. But the number was not large, and both sides approached the problem in a co-operative spirit. Able, sensible men in both countries—Robert Liston for example, the British minister in America from 1796 to 1800—helped to make the rapprochement a reality. With the peace of Amiens between Britain and France in 1802 there was a temporary easing of international tension.

America had weathered two major crises. She was now to reap the benefit of her special position in the world. Europe's mistakes were to be her opportunities. However, at the outset this particular opportunity seemed rather a potential disaster for the United States. What happened was that in France a brilliant thirty-year-old general, Napoleon Bonaparte, seized power in 1799. Declaring that the revolution had accomplished its mission and was therefore ended, he launched out on his fantastic career of imperial conquest. Foiled by the British in his descent on Egypt, Bonaparte turned his fertile mind to the possibilities in North America. One part of his plan involved the suppression of the Negro slave revolt in Haiti, a French possession in the West Indies. With peace restored in Haiti, the island could be used as a base for further operations. The other part of the plan concerned the immense territory known as Louisiana, between the Mississippi and the Rocky Mountains. Louisiana, as the names of its settlements (St. Louis, Baton Rouge, New Orleans) still recall, was in French hands until the Seven Years' War, when it was ceded to Spain. Napoleon was able to persuade the Spanish king to return Louisiana to France by secret treaty in 1800, offering in exchange a principality in conquered Italy. He pledged himself not to dispose of Louisiana to any other power.

The news of his acquisition reached America in 1801. It was enough to alarm the most complacent of Americans. Anything might happen once the impetuous genius of Napoleon occupied itself with the New World: the establishment of the French in Spanish Florida, the reconquest of Canada, the wresting of their trans-Appalachian wilderness from the as yet weak grasp of the Americans.

Jefferson feared that, as a preliminary stage, the French would close the Mississippi to United States commerce. Any power that held New Orleans, he wrote in 1802, must be "our natural and habitual enemy. . . . France, placing herself in that door, assumes to us the attitude of defiance." He did not dispute the French claim to the unexplored terrain beyond the Mississippi, but it seemed to him essential that the United States should control the mouth of the river. In other words, she must purchase New Orleans and the Floridas (which Jefferson assumed were also part of the Franco-Spanish agreement, and which then stretched as far west as the Mississippi). Congress was ready to appropriate $2 million for the purpose, and more could be found if need be.

This was at the beginning of 1803, when Jefferson chose his friend James Monroe as minister plenipotentiary to go to Paris and make the offer. He had already instructed the American minister in France, Robert R. Livingston, to present less ambitious proposals. When Monroe reached Paris in April, the situation had dramatically changed. The rebellion in Haiti was still smoldering and had proved so expensive to stamp out that Napoleon was weary of it. Now emperor and absolute ruler of France, he reacted with characteristic suddenness. He would renew the war in Europe and, concentrating his forces there, would forget the old French dream of American overlordship. France needed funds. If the United States could pay enough, she could have Louisiana; there was nothing Spain could do except protest.

So Livingston and Monroe, to their delight and astonishment, instead of having to bargain for New Orleans and the Floridas, were offered the whole of Louisiana. New Orleans was included in the bargain; Talleyrand was deliberately vague on the status of the Floridas, which actually remained Spanish. For a total of $15 million, the United States made the Louisiana Purchase, thereby doubling her area. The precise boundaries of the purchase were not determined, partly out of French evasiveness and partly because they never had been accurately fixed. Nor was the constitutionality of the acquisition altogether clear. Jefferson himself, a strict constructionist, was uneasy at what he had done, and Federalist opponents virtuously cited his own arguments against him. But these were relatively trivial matters that dwindled to nothing in face of the staggering prize which had fallen into American hands. The menace of Napoleonic ambition was abated at a stroke. So was the more permanent if less alarming danger of Spanish mischief. Providence must surely have a special fondness for the United States.

At least, an optimistic "Yanqui" could believe so in December, 1803, when—Spanish objections having been brushed aside—America took formal possession of Louisiana. Yet within a few years her worries appeared as great as ever. For one thing, her tremendous, unassimilated bulk offered temptations alike to discontented sectionalists and unscrupulous adventurers. Seeking to reverse what he regarded as unhealthy Federalist precedents, Jefferson provoked bitter partisan squabbles. Some New Englanders began to wonder whether they might not fare better by seceding from the Union and setting up a confederacy of northeastern states, bringing in New York if possible. In 1804–7 the mysterious Aaron Burr was concocting plans for a separate western domain. It is still uncertain whether he intended to carve this out of United States or Spanish territory, but there is no doubt that he was a man of singular craftiness or that his crony James Wilkinson, the American general who commanded in the Mississippi area, was in the pay of Spain. Whatever his plans, they came to nothing. But they were ominous symptoms.

Even more dismaying was the plight of neutral America in the renewed contest between France and England. All her initial grievances were multiplied to an insupportable degree. Victorious in the great naval battle off Cape Trafalgar (1805), Britain tightened its grip upon the high seas. Crushing state after state in whirlwind campaigns, Napoleon extended his mastery over the European continent. Since each major adversary was strong and tenacious, and neither could strike a mortal blow at the other, they turned to the indirect warfare of blockade and counterblockade.

Maintaining what was by far the largest navy in the world, as well as a considerable merchant marine, Britain was acutely short of sailors to man its fleets. Service in the Royal Navy was ill-paid, dangerous, and thankless. The desertion rate was high, especially into American ships, where conditions were much better. Deserters were encouraged by sympathetic Americans and in some cases provided with false naturalization papers. Other American seamen were British by birth, though not deserters. Whatever the status of the victims, British warships re-

sorted increasingly to their old custom of 1793–94—halting
American merchant vessels, searching them, and taking off any
man whom they judged to be British. This custom of impressment was infuriating to Americans for several reasons, not least
because in justifying it the British maintained the rule of "in-
defeasible allegiance": once a British citizen, always a British
citizen, whether deserter or emigrant. It was a familiar notion
in common law, but impugned the concept of independent
American sovereignty. In 1807 insult and injury were com-
pounded when the British frigate *Leopard,* in pursuit of alleged
deserters, fired a broadside into the United States frigate *Chesapeake,* killing or wounding twenty-one of the crew. It was a
"black outrage," in Secretary of State James Madison's words.
To halt any American ship was thought objectionable; to halt
a warship was unprecedented; to open fire on her was unpar-
donable. Though flagrantly at fault, the British delayed repara-
tion for over four years, using their obligation to pay as a diplomatic bargaining point. If the United States had been
equipped for war in 1807, the incident would probably have
caused it.

But Jefferson, struggling to avoid an outcome so repugnant
to his beliefs, tried every expedient short of war. Again the
British behaved with obstinate pugnacity, and again they had
reasons for doing so. Until 1805 they interpreted the rights of
neutral commerce with reasonable generosity. But then, shut
out from Napoleon's Continental System, their own commerce
and industry in danger of being throttled, they sought to retaliate. Napoleon's own supplies must be cut off; American ships
must be forbidden to bring goods to Europe from French and
Spanish colonies. Large numbers of American vessels engaged
in the traffic were peremptorily seized, their cargoes liable to

confiscation. Jefferson's protests met with no response. Nor did his intermittent experiments from 1806 onward at punishing England through non-importation schemes. He met with another failure when American emissaries sent to draw up a fresh agreement with England won no concessions and even gave ground. The resulting treaty, which reached America in March, 1807, was so ignominious that Jefferson withheld it from the Senate.

Britain would not budge; at least the United States could not budge her. The French were almost equally uncompromising, but their offense seemed less. They did not impress American seamen; their ships did not hover theateningly outside American harbors; and thanks to the tongue-in-cheek guile of Napoleon, their own later seizures of American shipping were to be conducted with a show of legality. They watched with a certain amusement when at the end of 1807 Jefferson and Madison tried a new tack, the Embargo.

It was a drastic device, an attempt both to assert American isolation and to retaliate against the European belligerents by prohibiting virtually all trade between the United States and other nations within the orbit of conflict. The effects of the Embargo were catastrophic. Many American merchants and mariners saw themselves deprived of a livelihood, though a few manufacturers rejoiced at the opportunity thrown their way. Others avoided ruin by flouting the law; smuggling into Canada was active, and so was illicit trade with the West Indies. In New England and New York, where maritime communities were hardest hit, there was violent hostility to the President's well-meant plan. The only gainers, said his critics, were the belligerents themselves; Americans—or, rather, some Americans —were being punished for the sins of Europe. Bowing to criticism, as one of his last presidential gestures in 1809 Jefferson signed legislation that repealed the Embargo Act in favor of a milder program of "non-intercourse."

Non-importation was ineffectual, embargo disastrous; non-intercourse—the reopening of trade with all nations except Britain and France, with a pledge to resume trade with the two offenders as soon as they mended their ways—solved few problems either. Jefferson's successor, James Madison—"poor Jemmy! . . . a withered little apple-John," as the writer Washington Irving saw him in 1811—inherited a sort of permanent crisis. Eight years as Jefferson's Secretary of State had taught him that there were no easy solutions. Through bad luck and some clumsy exchanges in which both English and American diplomatists were at fault, Madison's administration led from bad to worse. Concessions were accepted before they had been properly offered, withdrawn before properly rejected. Ill feeling, gleefully exploited by Napoleon, intensified.

Once the Republican leaders had thought Britain and France equally culpable. Now Britain was *the* enemy. It seemed that what Madison called her "hostile inflexibility" could not be modified by any means short of war and that there would be positive advantages to war. War would release resentments that had become painful to contain. War would be a simplification of intolerable complexities, indeed, a solution—the only solution. Moreover, according to the "war hawks" from the West and South who suddenly became influential in Congress during 1810–11, Canada would be America's reward for intervention. The British in Canada, as Henry Clay and other "war hawks" maintained (with some cause), were inciting the Indians of the Northwest: witness the confederacy just organized by the able Shawnee chief Tecumseh. In an open war the Indians would be crushed. Canada would provide them with no sanctuary, for Canada would be overrun by the avenging Americans. In fact, the American Revolution would not be complete until all British territories in North America had become incorporated in the United States. Also, England, fighting hard in the Spanish peninsula against French forces, was now allied with Spain. In 1810 the United States had already, with slightly dubious right, annexed the Spanish province of West Florida. If there were war with Britain, East Florida likewise would fall into American hands.

In addition to these views and the real grievances of seizure and impressment, which were more important causes, the maladroitness of Anglo-American diplomacy was a factor in bringing on the war. So was the duplicity of Napoleon's diplomacy. He half-persuaded the United States that he had canceled his regulations restricting neutral trade (the Berlin and Milan Decrees) and that the equivalent British Orders in Council had therefore no purpose except anti-Americanism. In fact, he had not ceased to maintain his Continental System, and in fact the British did belatedly suspend their Orders in Council on June 16, 1812. The date is significant, for after a fortnight of debate Congress finally decided to implement Madison's war message. War was declared against England on June 18, two days after the main pretext had been removed—though the Americans did not know it.

The War of 1812 was in many respects a fiasco. Begun for mixed motives, it dragged on for more than two years in an atmosphere of deepening gloom, even more unpopular in New England and New York than the Embargo had been. The nation's finances became chaotic. Military organization, especially at the outset, was pathetically inadequate. Of three expeditions that set out to invade Canada in 1812, two were rendered useless by the refusal of the militia contingents to leave their own state or to cross the boundary into Canada, while the third resulted in the needless surrender of two thousand American troops.

For a while, each month appeared to provide the Federalist opposition with fresh evidence that "Mr. Madison's war" was a fatal error. By 1814 things were both better and worse. Several able young military leaders, including Winfield Scott of Virginia, were found, and there were some engagements in which the Americans carried the day. American gunnery and naval design proved superior in a number of ship-versus-ship encounters. In naval battles on Lake Erie (September, 1813) and Lake Champlain (September, 1814) their success was equally marked, and of far greater strategic significance. A British descent on Baltimore was repulsed in September, 1814.

Other sides of the story were less heroic. The attack on Baltimore followed a humiliating raid on Washington in August, when the British set fire to the Capitol and the White House. The dream of Canadian conquest had faded. The enemy was occupying part of the Massachusetts province of Maine. Despite the victory of the United States *Constitution* over the British *Guerrière* and *Java*, or of the *United States* over the *Macedonian,* these frigate contests and the exploits of American privateers did nothing to break the crippling blockade of American ports. By the autumn of 1814, moreover, the war in Europe was at last over and Napoleon a prisoner. British troops were on their way from battlefields of the Old World to provide the New World with fresh cause for lamentation. One expedition, commanded by Sir Edward Pakenham, brother-in-law of the renowned Duke of Wellington, was about to undertake the capture of New Orleans.

At Ghent in Belgium, meanwhile, Anglo-American peace commissioners were in session. Both sides were anxious to terminate the contest. Their deliberations were protracted, however, since neither had secured a decisive superiority. Each modified its terms week by week, according to the latest news from America. In the outcome, neither was able to impose terms, and the treaty signed on Christmas Eve, 1814, settled nothing. Impressment and the other factors enumerated by Madison in his original war message to Congress were not even mentioned in the Treaty of Ghent. The final irony, it might be thought, was that Andrew Jackson's army shattered the British outside New Orleans in January, 1815, when the peace had already been concluded. Was even that triumph futile? Was the War of 1812 nothing more than a botched and jeopardized affair covered over by the pride and relief of that final, sensational, unnecessary battle?

Not altogether. It is easy enough to criticize Jefferson's misplaced idealism and to poke fun at his reliance upon unseaworthy gunboats as a defensive naval arm. Madison's handling of events, when Secretary of State and when President, can be questioned. But it is easier to show where they erred than what they should have done instead. Again and again they reviewed the alternatives. The most extreme possibility was war with Britain *and* France. This they rightly rejected as absurd. The tamest move, one recommended by the Federalists, was submission. This too they rightly rejected; it was likely to lead to more trouble, not less trouble. What in between? No verbal protest had any use. No punitive restriction of commerce hurt the warring nations as much as it did the neutral United States.

At the time and in the special circumstances there were quite cogent reasons for going to war with England. The United States conducted the war with such ineptitude that she was lucky to escape so lightly. But England and Canada were also lucky. They recognized as much. America *was* a hard enemy to beat, Canada *was* vulnerable; henceforward it would be preferable to reach understanding at the conference table. After 1815 there was considerable dislike of America in Britain; yet, diplomatically speaking, friendship was the policy. From England the cabinet ministers Castlereagh and Canning, whatever their private vexation, worked sincerely to fashion a lasting peace.

If the Treaty of Ghent settled nothing, it opened the way to future settlements. The various disputes that it merely noted and deferred for discussion by joint commissions were one by one taken up and in most cases sensibly decided. The Rush-Bagot Agreement (1817) restricted naval forces on Lake Champlain, Lake Ontario, and the Great Lakes to a token total of four small vessels on each side. With one or two exceptions, the entire Canadian-American frontier was determined by other agreements, along what are still roughly the present lines. There were conflicting claims to the ill-defined area of Oregon, bounded to the south by Spanish California and to the north by Russian Alaska. In 1818 Britain and the United States agreed to leave Oregon open for settlement by both parties for a ten-year period. The arrangement was renewed in 1827. Even the Newfoundland fisheries, perennially in dispute, were regulated in 1818, though so ambiguously that the controversy continued.

The War of 1812 was to be America's last serious external crisis for a century to come. At its conclusion the United States began to collect the rewards that followed automatically from her growing strength and from her geographical isolation. No one, save in a general world war, could seriously harm her. She in turn wished no harm to anyone, unless now and then for a temporary reason. After 1815—in which eventful year American warships also settled the old score with the Mediterranean pirate kingdoms—she could turn inward to the affairs of her own continent, reducing her regular military and naval establishments far beyond the point that a European power would have dared to approach. Even so, she had enough amateur military talent in 1818–19 to occupy East Florida, in pursuit of troublesome Seminole Indians, and enough diplomatic self-confidence to compel Spain to cede the area (by the Adams-Onís Treaty). The United States now possessed the whole of Florida as then defined, from the east bank of the Mississippi to the Atlantic coast. As for Spain, the great empire founded over three centuries by the conquistadors was tumbling to pieces; province after province was achieving and proclaiming independence. In 1821 the United States began formally to recognize her Latin American neighbors as sovereign republics.

The new situation in the American hemisphere created new flurries in international diplomacy, as revealed at the Congress of Verona in November, 1822. Spain, though divided by liberal-conservative feuds, was naturally anxious to recover her lost colonies. France, restored to the prim orthodoxy of Bourbon monarchy, was eager to lead the way. Tsar Alexander of Russia, architect of the "Holy Alliance," apparently was ready to lend active support. Prussia and Austria, or at any rate their rulers, declared their attachment to the legitimist cause and their corresponding hatred of revolution. Only Britain held aloof. However tyrannical in American eyes, however conservative in her ruling class, England was the most liberal of the European nations, although hers was a liberalism interlaced with commerce. She had established close economic ties with Latin America and had every reason to expect that they could be drawn still closer.

It seems unlikely that France would actually have gone so far as to mount a military expedition against the self-styled republics of Spanish America. But contemporaries took the threat seriously, and the two powers most affected by it were Britain and the United States. Though Britain had not yet officially recognized the new nations, that was only a matter of time. In other respects her responses were akin to those of the United States. Neither wished to see European powers intervene in the affairs of the American hemisphere; each was prepared to take a firm line in opposing such intervention. British naval and United States military strength would provide formidable obstacles to any rescue operation launched from the Old World.

Anglo-American co-operation was one element in the equation, the one that the British Foreign Secretary, George Canning, stressed in 1823 when he approached the American minister in London with a suggestion that the two countries might make a joint declaration, so as to discourage any possible move by Tsar Alexander's Holy Alliance. The idea was attractive to James Monroe, who had replaced Madison in the White House in 1817. The last of the "Virginia dynasty" of presidents, and an old hand though not always a fortunate one at diplomacy, Monroe consulted his compeers Jefferson and Madison. They were of his opinion: co-operation was the right plan.

But there was another element in the equation—Anglo-American rivalry—and this was the one stressed by Monroe's equally experienced Secretary of State, John Quincy Adams.

The Nation Takes Shape

The very fact that their interests overlapped was for him proof that the United States should beware. Adams knew almost every corner of Europe. He had been minister to the Netherlands in 1794–97, to Prussia in 1797–1801, to Russia in 1809–14, to England in 1815–17, and one of the commissioners at Ghent in 1814. Everything in European diplomacy—the customary 10 per cent *douceur* or "sweetener" to officials, the more blatant, outright bribes, the aristocratic protocol—he took as evidence of a corruption from which America must keep clear. He deeply mistrusted British motives, suspecting British as well as Russian designs upon the Oregon region. So he persuaded Monroe to make a unilateral declaration of American policy, leaving Canning's proposal severely alone.

The President duly announced what became known as the Monroe Doctrine (though John Quincy Adams deserves to be honored as its chief author) during the course of his annual message to Congress in December, 1823. The American hemisphere, he said, would not henceforth be considered open to colonization by European powers, though the United States would not interfere with existing European possessions in the New World or concern herself with the internal affairs of European nations.

Monroe's remarks formed only a portion of his address. They did not constitute a treaty or a contribution to international law. They were simply an expression of American sentiment. The "doctrine" was not very impressive to Europe as a whole, though it gained some approval in England and aroused some alarm elsewhere—not for what the United States threatened to do but because of the subversive tone of the message: it might have a bad influence. Its immediate results were negligible. Canning had already secured a promise from the French that they would stay out of America, and the Latin American countries still relied mainly upon Britain. Their faith seemed justified in the following year, when Britain formally recognized their independence, and again in 1826, when Britain participated in a Pan-American conference—the first ever held—at Panama. The United States was in such political discord by then that her two delegates were not appointed until it was too late. Even if they had attended the conference they could have accomplished little, so reluctant were their fellow countrymen to be committed to any form of international agreement—especially one that raised awkward sectional issues in connection with slavery.

The Monroe Doctrine, as first announced, is not so important for what it achieved as for what it revealed of underlying American attitudes to foreign policy. Everything in the doctrine was implicit at the beginning of American independence. It amounted to a restatement in more sweeping terms of what had already been said in Washington's Farewell Address and in a dozen other less celebrated documents. Thus John Adams declared in a special message to Congress (1797): "We ought not to involve ourselves in the political system of Europe, but to keep ourselves always distinct and separate from it." Other presidents used similar language. American diplomatists, in speaking of Louisiana, put forward a distinct though as yet not fully avowed American claim to pass judgment on transfers of territory within North America. Jefferson summed up much discussion, and incidentally reiterated some of his own words, when replying to Monroe's request for advice in October, 1823:

Our first and fundamental maxim should be, never to entangle ourselves in the broils of Europe; our second, never to suffer Europe to intermeddle with cis-Atlantic affairs. America, North and South, has a set of interests distinct from those of Europe. . . . She should therefore have a system of her own, separate . . . from that of Europe. While the last is laboring to become the domicile of despotism, our endeavor should surely be, to make our hemisphere that of freedom.

Such was the background of the Monroe Doctrine. As the incidents of this decade and the next demonstrated, however, American foreign policy was not yet cast in a complete or coherent pattern. For one thing, Anglo-American relations remained equivocal. In 1823 John Quincy Adams convinced Monroe that a joint move would be a mistake. We may agree. Or we may be swayed by the argument of some historians who picture the affair as a great opportunity for Anglo-American friendship thrown away. Perhaps the latter view seeks to mold the past too much according to the patterns of the present. Certainly Britain continued to occupy a special place in American thought. She was hated, suspected, admired—and even loved: the most likely enemy in the event of another war, and yet the most obvious ally in terms of strategy and of emotional kinship. Co-operation with Britain seemed both essential and inconceivable. The United States, for example, ended the importation of slaves in 1808. Thereafter she became associated with England in patrolling the slave coast of West Africa. But for the patrol to be effective, the policing ships (nearly all British) must be granted the right to halt and search other vessels. How could such a right be accorded, when it was one of the reasons for America's entry into the War of 1812? Yet how could it be denied?

Though the Monroe Doctrine prescribed isolation within the American continent, the United States could never achieve perfect isolation. She was linked with Britain and the rest of the world; the link was reaffirmed every time an American ship put into a foreign harbor, anywhere from Bristol to Bombay. Yet within her own hemisphere the United States achieved almost too thorough an isolation. The Panama conference would have failed despite American attendance, but in any case the hemisphere "system" of which Jefferson spoke was for long to remain an oddly unreal basis for an allegedly practical foreign policy.

Neither could the Monroe Doctrine take account of other considerations: for instance, the extent to which the formulation of foreign policy would lie at the mercy of domestic events. The latent conflict between executive and Senate had already caused some embarrassment. More serious was the effect of partisan policies in dividing the President from the legislature. John Quincy Adams' single term in the White House, from 1825 to 1829, was made wretched by hostility in Congress. Skilled though he was in diplomacy, he did not enjoy the effort of conducting it in the midst of Washington's special brand of domestic intrigue. He failed, for instance, to persuade Britain to widen her concessions to American trade in the West Indies.

His successor, Andrew Jackson, had better luck with the British, in 1830. And Jackson by hectoring methods compelled the French to pay some old outstanding claims. Why was he successful? Not entirely, or even principally, because of his truculence, but rather because other extraneous circumstances induced the British and French to give way. American diplomacy was, indeed, characterized by brutal directness. Adams himself specialized in asperity, and by 1837 Americans had grown accustomed to thinking that their negotiators should make *no* concession. "Freedom" must not yield to "despotism."

The Nation Takes Shape

Any American who compromised at the conference table must be a dupe. In the perpetual, oversimplified dualism of American opinion, Europe was not only wrong but wickedly wrong, the United States not only right but shiningly so. This belief, in the resentment it aroused, accounts for some of the anti-Americanism exhibited by European statesmen and others.

The United States still had much to learn. Her foreign policy had not been thoroughly thought out. Some of her gains had been fortuitous. Some of her difficulties had been self-imposed. She had stated various principles on which policy was based, but there were inherent dangers and contradictions in these principles. In 1837 America was still regarded by the European powers as something of an upstart. If she persisted in describing them as satanic agencies, they could return the compliment by excluding her from their intellectual systems. To the French sociologist Auguste Comte, for example, what he named the "Great Western Republic," as late as 1848, was not the United States, but the "five civilized nations"—Britain, France, Spain, Italy, and Germany. They constituted the civilized world of the mind in his reckoning. Only the radicals in Europe took America at her own valuation.

Nevertheless, the United States had come a long way in fifty years. She had upheld her neutrality in most trying circumstances and vindicated her nationality in the mercifully brief War of 1812. The toughness of her diplomatists—the two Adamses were of exceptional caliber—had paid well in practice. Her frontiers were secure, her prospects boundless. She had escaped from the one alliance to which she was committed. Britain was still the most powerful nation in the world, but not even Britain had as much real or figurative room for maneuver and expansion. She could afford to neglect foreign relations, and even afford the luxury of mistakes in diplomacy. "Lucky America," a European might sigh; for him the word "frontier" meant a line of armed truce, a constant potential threat of war. A less generous European might say sourly that America was her own worst enemy. Perhaps so. Yet both comments emphasized the cardinal fact that she had no external enemy to fear—nothing but oceans and mountains to east and west, nothing but peaceable Canada to the north and the rearranged fragments of the Spanish Empire to the southwest and south.

IV

The West: Territorial and Agricultural Expansion

In his first inaugural address (1801), President Thomas Jefferson congratulated his fellow citizens on their possession of "a chosen country, with room enough for our descendants to the thousandth and thousandth generation." Two years later, by the Louisiana Purchase, the area of the chosen country was doubled and not long afterward again augmented by the half-conquest, half-purchase of Florida. In view of Jefferson's words, one might have thought that the United States owned more land than it knew what to do with. After all, in over a hundred and fifty years of colonial occupation, the line of white settlement had at hardly any point penetrated more than three hundred miles from the Atlantic coast, and in many areas less than that: two miles per annum, on a rough average. When Washington became President, the Appalachian Mountains marked the limit of successful settlement except in the western regions of Virginia and Pennsylvania.

The West

Yet within another half-century the frontier had pushed inland—north, west, and south—for over a thousand miles at its farthest extent. The advance, according to the astonished Tocqueville, was proceeding at an average of seventeen miles per annum. State after state had been created out of the wilderness, to join the original thirteen. Others were emerging. Nor were Americans content to remain inside the undisputed borders of their land. Starting in 1821, when Mexico secured independence and invited American settlement, they began to flock into the Mexican province of Texas. By 1836 the "Yanqui" Texans were numerous enough to break away from Mexico, and to sustain *their* independence as the Lone Star Republic by force of arms. In the same decade, thousands of Americans were beginning to take the Oregon Trail, though the final status of Oregon was not to be determined until 1846.

Why so much and such swift activity? And how was it accomplished? It is to be explained in part as a world-wide phenomenon—the occupation of the empty spaces of other continents by the European peoples, a movement whose origins lay back in the fifteenth century. In the nineteenth century the momentum of expansion increased amazingly, until the white man was exploring and then consolidating his hold over every part of the globe. The trader, missionary, pioneer, soldier, made his way into Australia, Africa, the plains of central Asia, as well as into the American continent. Behind him were the technological and financial resources of a Europe whose population was growing at an unprecedented rate.

However, the process was nowhere more impressive than in the United States, where the rapidity of expansion appeared all the greater in contrast to the previous steady but modest progress of the thirteen colonies. In that earlier era various factors limited westward expansion. Though the numbers of American colonists multiplied, through immigration and through natural increase, their hands were fully occupied in carving out the thirteen seaboard commonwealths. Indian tribes—notably those of the powerful Iroquois confederation in western New York—were sometimes a serious deterrent to pioneering enterprise. The inland empire of the French, while not thickly garrisoned, could not be annexed without a long series of wars. British colonial policy was unsympathetic to ambitious plans for settlement beyond the Appalachians. The land itself, walled in to the west by ridge upon ridge of hills, its surface densely wooded and largely innocent of roads, its rivers unnavigable for large vessels beyond the fall line, where the smooth current broke into rapids—the land itself discouraged massive transfers of population.

Some of the impediments were removed by the War of Independence and the Treaty of Paris. In the absence of other hindrances, there were no international complications to prevent the Americans from pushing through the Appalachian passes and into the great Mississippi basin. But there were still local and national problems to solve. Most of them had to do with questions of landownership. At the outbreak of the Revolution seven of the thirteen colonies were laying claim to western territories, either under original "sea-to-sea" charters or through subsequent developments. The most ambitious assertions of territorial right were those of Virginia, which maintained that its ultimate boundaries embraced not only trans-Allegheny Kentucky but also the whole region north of the Ohio that was to be known as the Northwest Territory. New York also felt it had a title to the region north of the Ohio. The putative frontiers of Georgia and South Carolina likewise overlapped. Massachusetts, Connecticut, and North Carolina insisted that they too had been granted ownership of strips of land extending due west to the Mississippi—strips which in the case of Massachusetts and Connecticut lay within the theoretical domain of Virginia. New York and New Hampshire squabbled over possession of the province of Vermont.

The situation was further confused by a mass of individual land claims. Each state had promised bounty lands to its Revolutionary soldiers; some previous military grants had been made (George Washington, for example, was able to acquire several thousand acres from the area set aside to reward the Virginia veterans of the Seven Years' War); and considerable stretches of land had already been occupied by squatters or sold to pioneers and speculators.

Little by little the muddle was resolved, during the Revolutionary War and in the next few years, as the states ceded their western lands to the United States. "Military reserves" were set aside; otherwise, by degrees, the national government took title. The most decisive gesture of relinquishment was made by Virginia in 1784; thereafter Massachusetts, Connecticut, and the Carolinas fell into line. Georgia, her legislature involved in corrupt land deals, was the last to yield her tarnished title (in 1802) to the region that was to form the states of Alabama and Mississippi. A number of Indian tribal claims were meanwhile extinguished by coercion or negotiation.

Here then was an enormous western area available to settlement. Many of the best tracts—usually along the river bottoms —were already staked out. But there was land in abundance, waiting to be cleared, waiting to appreciate in value, waiting to make farmers happy and speculators delirious. The latter would get what price they could for their investment. But the public lands, it was determined by the Ordinance of 1785, would be sold in minimum lots of one square mile, or 640 acres, at $1 per acre. These lots would be surveyed rectangularly in checkerboard townships of thirty-six sections, each block six miles square. The township survey was not to be the universal pattern. However, it prevailed in many areas, and the price and unit of sale, though modified, were established as a basic formula.

Another ordinance, of 1787, served as a higher theorem in the geometry of expansion. This defined the triangle between the Ohio, Mississippi, and Great Lakes as the Northwest Territory. The territory was to have a governor and—when it reached a population of five thousand free, adult males—a legislature as well as a non-voting representative in Congress. It was to be divided eventually into somewhere between three and five states, each of which would initially qualify for territorial recognition and then become eligible for statehood within the Union when the free inhabitants numbered sixty thousand. Each new state would have perfect equality with the older ones. "Involuntary servitude"—slavery—was prohibited in the Northwest Territory (and the states later formed from it also decided not to permit slavery). This final prohibition did not apply to other frontier regions—to the Southwest Territory, for example, organized in 1790—but the ordinance as a whole prescribed a sequence of growth that was to control the settlement of the entire West. The Union, master but not tyrant of its infant territories, could multiply its members by orderly accretion and still remain in the Union. It was an admirable arrangement, worthy to be set beside that other great document of 1787, the Constitution.

In the half-dozen years that followed the adoption of the

Constitution, the prospects for western development were brightened in other ways. A few reasonably good turnpikes, or toll roads, were constructed, and some rougher trails began to reach out toward the upper Ohio and the settlements of Tennessee. A defeat inflicted by the Indians of the Northwest Territory upon American regulars and militia in 1791 was canceled out three years later, when "Mad Anthony" Wayne, the American commander in the territory, routed the enemy at Fallen Timbers, by the Maumee rapids of Ohio. His victory helped to bring about the Treaty of Greenville (1795), by which no less than twelve Indian tribes were forced to surrender title to a great stretch of their ancestral lands. Coupled with the meeting of crestfallen chiefs at Fort Greenville, Jay's Treaty of the same period put an end for a while to the danger of serious British intervention in the Northwest Territory. With the British gone from Niagara, Detroit, and elsewhere, in fulfilment of Jay's Treaty, the Indians had no longer the dream of sustenance by a powerful ally. Their own strength in war could not match that of the Americans. Finally, the diplomatic success of Pinckney's Treaty (1795) with Spain reassured the frontiersmen of the South.

The cumulative result was remarkable. As it happened, the first new state (and fourteenth in all) to join the Union was not on the western but on the northern frontier of the United States—Vermont, whose upper areas, like those of the neighboring and rival claimants New York and New Hampshire, were still mainly wilderness. The next states to be admitted were Kentucky (1792) and Tennessee (1796), lying across the Alleghenies from Virginia and North Carolina, respectively. Then came Ohio (1803), the first state carved from the Northwest Territory. Next—made rapidly eligible through the nucleus of French settlements—was Louisiana (1812). In the deep South between Louisiana and Georgia there were created the states of Mississippi (1817) and Alabama (1819). In the meantime, the Northwest Territory was again subdivided; to the west of Ohio came Indiana (1816), and west again Illinois (1818). Next was Maine (1820), a state created out of a state —Massachusetts—in the far northeast of the United States. With Maine was paired Missouri (1821), the first state to lie completely west of the Mississippi. From western Missouri to eastern Maine was a distance of some fifteen hundred miles. The boundaries of settlement stretched and stretched. Arkansas Territory, between Missouri and Louisiana, became a state in 1836; Michigan, a fourth state fashioned from the original Northwest Territory, gained full admission to the Union in 1837. Twenty-six states in all, half of them old colonial commonwealths and half of them created in the era from Washington's inauguration to that of Van Buren—the shape of the Union was being profoundly transformed.

The changed emphasis was reflected in the early careers of some of America's public men. Andrew Jackson, raised in the Carolinas, went off in 1788, at the age of twenty-one, to Nashville, Tennessee. Henry Clay, born not far from Richmond, Virginia, in 1777, migrated with his parents to Kentucky in 1792 and, after returning to Virginia to study law, crossed the Alleghenies once more as an enterprising youth of twenty to settle in Lexington, Kentucky. Thomas Hart Benton, born in 1782 in the North Carolina piedmont country (where his ancestors had moved from central Virginia), shifted with his family to Tennessee in 1801 and then in 1815 made a second emigration to St. Louis, Missouri. James K. Polk, a future President raised in Mecklenburg County, North Carolina, was eleven years old when his parents journeyed to the Duck River country of central Tennessee in 1806. Another President-to-be, Abraham Lincoln, was born in Kentucky and moved with his family to southern Indiana in 1816, when he was nearly eight years old, and on into Illinois in 1830. Lincoln's political rival, Stephen Douglas, grew up in Vermont and headed west in 1833 at the age of twenty, settling eventually in Jacksonville, Illinois. A less amenable rival of later years, Jefferson Davis, was born in Kentucky only a few months before Lincoln and only a few miles away from him. Davis' father, a native of Georgia, had come there in 1796. In about 1810 he uprooted himself again, traveling to Louisiana and settling soon after in Mississippi. Two men who had much to do with the American advance into Texas, Stephen F. Austin and Sam Houston, were both born in Virginia in 1793. Houston's family took him to Tennessee in 1807, Austin's to the Missouri region in 1808.

Such histories could be duplicated in thousands of other, more obscure cases. Beginning about 1795, after a generation of comparative immobility in which Americans had other things to grapple with, the frontier moved inland relentlessly. There was a pause during the War of 1812, but then the process was continued more swiftly than ever. We have described some of the mechanisms of settlement in broad outline; they deserve an explanation and then a closer look.

There were any number of negative reasons for expansion, that is, of reasons for dissatisfaction with existence in the seaboard states. Thus, in New England, which was fond of jesting—half in earnest—that its principal exports were rock and ice, farmers grew weary of struggling with stony, infertile acres. The valley agriculture of New England was prosperous enough, but much of New England was plateau and hillside, fit for subsistence farming only. By the end of the eighteenth century many a Yankee farmer was trekking west toward the pleasant valleys of western New York or the rich tracts of Ohio, where better land than that he had quitted was available at a fifth or even a tenth of the price. Again, taxation was not monstrously high in New England; yet it was something to be reckoned with, and certainly higher than the sums levied upon the settler in Ohio. The rule of the Congregational church and the Federalist party was not oppressive, at least not by European standards; yet it too was irksome to a Bible-reading Methodist or an ardent Republican.

In the middle colonies and the South similar reasons applied. The plight of the farmer in Maryland, Virginia, and North Carolina was more acute, since the fertility of his piedmont holdings was being disastrously reduced by erosion and exhaustion of the soil. He also found it harder and harder to survive with dignity in a society increasingly dominated by the large planter. The planter for his part, especially if his lands were in the older-established tidewater districts, suffered from the diminishing yields from tired, overexploited soil. Tobacco, for some time the staple in the upper South, was a particularly greedy crop; more enlightened planters, such as George Washington, attempted with varying success to remedy matters by the use of fertilizer or by turning from tobacco to wheat.

Confronted by such problems, the easterner was further induced to sell out and seek new land by the existence of improved or newly constructed routes to the interior. A New Englander, for example, could now drive his wagon and his livestock along passably good roads to the Hudson and thence via the Mohawk Valley to Lake Erie. A Pennsylvanian or Marylander could take advantage of the two old military roads—originally laid out in the Seven Years' War—that converged on Pittsburgh and so into the Ohio Valley. It was also possible for them and for Virginians to travel southwest via Richmond or via the Shenandoah Valley through Cumberland Gap to Kentucky, or by the Knoxville road into Tennessee. These were roads of a sort, but there were also various trails open to the hardy settler whose wagon was not too heavy laden. "Zane's Trace," a trail blazed in 1796 across Ohio, was a typical early route.

In consequence, Tennessee and Kentucky were peopled almost overnight. By 1796, when it became a state, Tennessee had seventy-seven thousand inhabitants. Four years later, Kentucky could claim a population of two hundred thousand. The occupation of frontier territories to the north was less simple, because of complicated land deals. Enormous tracts in Ohio and western New York were sold to companies of speculators, both by the states concerned and by holders of military bounty lands. Massachusetts disposed of a six-million-acre claim to Phelps and Gorham, two rich and influential jobbers, for what amounted to about three cents an acre. They in turn passed the Phelps-Gorham Purchase on to the New York speculator Robert Morris for some eight cents an acre. He added to this empire by buying the whole of what remained of westernmost New York. Lacking capital to develop the region himself and knowing that American resources were limited, he turned to those of Europe after setting aside a valuable zone for his own purposes. Part of what he offered was acquired by a syndicate of British capitalists, and an even larger area passed into the hands of Dutch bankers in Amsterdam. This group, the Holland Land Company, made extensive purchases elsewhere.

Each European syndicate attempted to "colonize" its holdings. Trees were cut down to form clearings, roads built, mills constructed, townships such as Bath, Cazenovia, and Utica laid out. Alluring circulars were distributed in eastern districts, announcing ready-made paradises on the frontier. The emigrant was of course expected to pay a higher price for these improved lands, but it seemed reasonable to assume that he would gladly do so.

The expectation was not wholly fulfilled. The European capitalists did not in the long run fare so badly as Robert Morris, who overreached himself, went bankrupt, and spent three thoughtful years in the Philadelphia debtors' prison. But they and Morris discovered that frontier settlement was a tricky affair. The speculator might make a fortune, but he had to be nimble, hardheaded, and not too grandiose. Western settlers, it became clear, did not want pre-established Arcadias. Or rather, they could not afford such luxuries. They did not object in principle to the scheme, though in fact the land companies wasted a good deal of money in unsound developments. The settlers, however, had more energy than cash. It suited them best to pay for developments in kind, through the sweat of their own brows. This was true despite the New England tendency to settle in compact townships, much like those laid out by the land companies' agents. So, while the Holland Company eventually sold its tracts at a reasonable profit and while the British capitalists also got a modest return, their notion of wholesale settlement was not to become characteristic in the development of the West. Capital was needed on the frontier, but not in this form.

The common style of settlement, as in colonial times, was that the first arrival—after the hunters and trappers—was a pioneer. He was poor, like Abraham Lincoln's father, and often shiftless. He cleared himself a patch of ground, planted a crop, grazed his hogs in the nearby forest, shot wild birds and animals for the larder, and usually moved on again in a few years. After these men came the steady farmers, the consolidators, who would have a proper legal title to their land, who would methodically clear it, and who would intend to stay put. The pioneer, since he had little or no money in hand, was often a squatter. The permanent settler who supplanted him was better placed. But neither was able to command much credit. Hence a growing demand in the West for cheaper land in smaller units and for more generous methods of payment.

Western agitation met with some success. In 1800, land policy was modified so as to permit the settler to buy 320 acres (where previously 640 acres had been the unit of sale), though at a minimum price of $2 per acre, and to purchase his half-section over a four-year period. In 1804 the half-section was reduced to a quarter-section; an emigrant could now buy 160 acres of government land for $320, paying for it at the manageable rate of $80 a year. In 1820 he lost this credit opportunity but gained in other ways, since the new law allowed a minimum purchase of only 80 acres at $1.25 per acre in cash. And in 1832, additional legislation provided for the sale of public lands in 40-acre lots at $1.25 an acre. The fifty-dollar settler was likely to find himself on indifferent land, with a holding that kept him busy but which was not large enough to furnish a rich living. The more prudent and prosperous emigrant could look forward to a superior existence; yet even he had his worries. He had to reckon upon an outlay of several hundred dollars—the initial cost of the land, the expense of clearing it, digging a well, buying and planting seed for his wheat or corn, building a house, constructing fences and barns—before he was well established. Within five years, if things went smoothly, he could be firmly ensconced. But he was not insured against calamity; bad harvests, ill-health, an economic depression (such as that of 1819) could wreck his high hopes. By and large, however, the man who moved west was glad he had done so.

Perhaps it is misleading to think of any such "typical" figure. Different geographical zones produced different kinds of settlers, with varying occupations. The wheat-farmer of the Old Northwest shaded southward by degrees into the corn-raising yeoman, and so south again to the Kentuckian with his crop of hemp or tobacco, and then again south to what was to be the greatest American agricultural staple of all—cotton. Cotton had been produced in the South before the Revolutionary War, along with indigo, rice, and sugar, but until the 1790's it was dwarfed in importance by tobacco. Then the situation was revolutionized by the prodigious growth of the British cotton textile industry, by the resultant expansion of demand for raw cotton, and by the celebrated cotton "gin" of Eli Whitney. This young man from Massachusetts, observing on a visit to the South that the separation of the ordinary short-staple cotton fiber from its seed was a laborious and expensive hand operation, invented a simple device that would do the work mechanically in a fraction of the time. Like most pioneers in technology, he got little or no financial benefit from his invention. But he altered the whole economy of the South by rendering the large-scale cultivation of cotton not only feasible but temptingly lucrative. Cotton provided the impetus for the expansion of the southwestern frontier and determined its particular character.

For cotton was thought to depend ultimately upon slave labor. So long as it was a crop of limited usefulness, there was a good prospect of ending the institution of slavery in the whole United States. Outstanding southerners of Revolutionary times—a Washington, a Jefferson, or a George Mason—regarded slavery as a misfortune fastened upon their section. They feared the consequences of its unchecked spread and were ready to follow the northern states in systems of gradual emancipation. But when the demand for cotton became virtually unlimited and it was clear that the supply also could be increased to an almost unlimited degree, then slavery by successive stages came to appear as a necessary evil, as an inevitable concomitant of plantation life, and, by about 1830, as no longer an evil or even an embarrassment but a positive good, an integral part of southern civilization.

So cotton cultivation started in the 1790's to reach west from the seaboard, across the Virginia and Carolina piedmont. It was not confined to large plantations. The rich planter was always greatly outnumbered in the South by the small slaveholder, and the latter by the little farmer who owned no slaves. But the successful planter—often a self-made man, a "first-generation" aristocrat—dominated the southern economy of the early nineteenth century, as he has dominated the southern mythology ever since. His profits were bigger than those of yeoman farmers, his means correspondingly more ample. By degrees he bought out the minor agriculturist in all the best farming areas.

The nationwide process of expansion was both interrupted and facilitated by the War of 1812. From the westerner's point of view the war's chief virtue was in the suppression of Indian risings. William Henry Harrison, the governor of Indiana Territory, made a start in 1811 when he fought an inconclusive battle with Tecumseh's Shawnee warriors at Tippecanoe. Two years later, at the Battle of the Thames, Harrison defeated the Shawnee confederacy and their British allies. It was a small battle, in which less than twenty white men were killed on each side, but it was decisive; Tecumseh was among the slain, and his downfall shattered the British-Indian alliance in the Northwest. In the Southwest—in southern Alabama—the militia general Andrew Jackson crushed the insurgent Creek Indians in several ferocious encounters. Even before these campaigns the Indians had ceased to be anything but a local and temporary menace to white settlement. After them, the dispirited tribes gave way, ceding their territories and withdrawing across the Mississippi into reservations allotted by the federal government.

Up to 1837 there were only two more Indian wars, each of which could and should have been avoided. The national government's Indian policy varied from President to President. From the time of Monroe it envisaged the gradual transfer of Indian tribes to their new western areas, after fair purchase of their old lands and with assistance in making the journey. The state governments, however, were less patient; the individual western settler was fiercely intolerant; and both were encouraged in their efforts to oust the Indian by the knowledge that President Jackson felt as they did. Their attitude is conveyed in words written by George Lepner about 1830 (and published posthumously by the *Southern Literary Messenger* in 1837). "How sickening," he said, "are the sentimental effusions upon the subject of the 'poor Indians' . . . . [T]he savage must ever recede before the man of civilization. . . . The square mile which furnishes game to a single family of hunters, will support a thousand families by agriculture and the mechanic arts, of which agriculture is the parent. . . . The savage who will not earn his subsistence, after the diminution of game, in the way that Providence prescribed, has the right of way upon the soil, and nothing more, until the agriculturist appears for whom it was intended."

The argument might have seemed inapplicable to the Five Civilized Tribes of the Southwest—Cherokee, Creek, Chickasaw, Choctaw, and Seminole—who were themselves peaceful "agriculturists." A few of these Indians were rich men. One Choctaw chieftain, Greenwood Laflore, had four hundred Negro slaves on his cotton plantation and spent $10,000 to furnish the salon of his Mississippi mansion with elegant French chairs, tables, mirrors, and carpeting. But their lands, which covered great tracts of western Georgia, eastern Alabama, Tennessee, northern Mississippi, and Florida, were eagerly sought by white settlers; and eventually the hapless Indians were displaced. All, that is, except the Seminoles, who resisted the invasion of their Florida reservation. From 1833 until the last flicker of intermittent conflict in 1842 they fought a tenacious guerrilla war in the swamps of Florida. But they too were doomed. By the end of Jackson's presidency virtually all the major tribes had lost their former lands and retreated forlornly westward to the Indian districts parceled out for them beyond the limits of white settlement in Arkansas, Mis-

souri, and the upper Mississippi. They had lost the day, forever. This was true of the northern as well as the southern
border; the embittered Sauk and Fox Indians, led by their
elderly chief Black Hawk, were provoked into one final tragi-
comic "war" along the Illinois frontier in 1832. They too
were cleared from the path of white settlement. No less than
ninety-four Indian treaties were negotiated during Jackson's
eight years of office, and millions of acres passed from the
savage to the man of civilization.

At this point it is interesting again to ask why the westward
impulse continued to be strong after the War of 1812. Some
of the answers have already been suggested; all seemed to be
reinforced after 1815. In the Southwest the cotton kingdom
was the prime absorber of new land, partly because of the
insatiable world demand for cotton and partly because there
was an alarming deterioration in the crop yield from older
areas of settlement. The construction of military and other
highways encouraged the hesitating emigrant to filter into
central Alabama by the Great Valley Road from Virginia and
the Carolinas or to stream into Mississippi along the trail from
Nashville, Tennessee, to Natchez. Government land offices
disposed of so much property in boom years—seven million
dollars worth in Huntsville, Alabama, in 1818—that "doing a
land-office business" entered the popular idiom as an image
of frantic commercial activity. The invention of the steamboat, convincingly tested by Robert Fulton at New York in
1807 and swiftly adapted for use on shallow inland waterways,
did much to stimulate settlement. By 1820 half of America's
cotton was grown in the newly developed gulf plains, and
nearly half the population of those burgeoning territories consisted of Negro slaves. At the other end of the social scale

from the planter with his substantial investment in slaves came the poor white, scratching an existence from soil too thin to nourish cotton.

On the central and northern frontier the pace of western settlement was quickened by the growing world market for grain, by immigration, and by improved transportation. Perhaps 200,000 permanent immigrants entered the United States between 1790 and 1820. In the following decade over 140,000 came in, and another 400,000 arrived in the years 1831–37. Most were from Ireland, Germany, and Britain. Some came with enough funds to purchase good land, and a high proportion moved inland. Many of them had cause to praise the Erie Canal, begun by New York in 1817 and completed in 1825, a spectacularly ambitious and successful enterprise that opened a smooth water highway all the way from New York City to the Erie shore of Ohio. The immigrants who remained close to the ports of entry—Boston, New York, Philadelphia—perforce entered the less congenial kinds of employment. Possibly this helped to release prospective native settlers.

Yet when all the certainties and possibilities have been added up, there is an extra element of passion—one might call it obsession—about the opening of the American frontier that cannot be fully understood in the language of logic or necessity. No doubt, as Frederick Jackson Turner and other American historians have maintained, the extension of the West was an experience that held profound significance for Americans. One clue to its character is provided by Jefferson. In 1801 he said that there was abundant room in the United States. But in that address he was anxious to be conciliatory, to dwell on America's harmony and blessings, not on her stresses and strains. In 1786, on the other hand, he noted that the inhabited portions of the United States had a population density of ten persons to the square mile, and "wherever we reach that the inhabitants become uneasy, as too much compressed, and go off in great numbers to search for vacant country." At the present rate of expansion, he calculated, all the territory east of the Mississippi would be occupied within forty years, that is, by 1826. He anticipated that Americans would then push beyond the Mississippi and into South America as well.

There was nothing unusual in Jefferson's opinion, though he was more perceptive than most and more intellectually curious. Nearly all Americans would have done as he did in snapping up the French offer of Louisiana. Not all would have been as resourceful as he was in sending out the Lewis and Clark expedition of 1804–6 to explore the northwestern reaches of the continent. But as a whole his countrymen thoroughly approved of such activities, even if Congress was niggardly in voting funds for some subsequent explorations. Jefferson represented an American dream of potentiality that was almost boundless. Its mathematics were theoretical, for all their air of exactitude; they appealed to the future, to the ultimate destinies of the young nation, combining foresightedness and fantasy in proportions that were hard to distinguish from one another.

Thus the census figures showed that the population of the United States had grown by more than a third each decade and had therefore more than doubled in a thirty-year period: it was 3,930,000 in 1790; 5,310,000 in 1800; 7,240,000 in 1810; 9,640,000 in 1820; 12,870,000 in 1830; and 17,070,000 by 1840. This geometric progression was assumed to be almost a natural law, and American notions of land needs were predicated upon the expectation of a sustained and prodigious increase in population. So, while a Jefferson might base his calculations of ten people to the square mile on the abundance of land, a Lepner might—in forecasting the wildly unlikely dependence of a thousand families on each square mile—rest his case upon the idea that there could never be too much land to meet the eventual requirements of the giant republic. In such a way could the pessimistic doctrines of Malthus be made to serve the optimistic drives of western expansion. By any customary standard, America was unbelievably rich in land resources. There was no strict need for New Englanders to emigrate after the bad summer and hard winter of 1816–17, or for the settlers of Georgia to appropriate Indian territories. As the older states pointed out in vain, conditions were quite tolerable within their boundaries. Soil depletion would not have occurred if farmers had been more careful, and it could still be halted if more intelligence were shown. Nor were the immigrants from Europe all as impoverished as legend would have us believe. The ships laden with them and the wagon trains and canal barges that bore them west together with native emigrants were not fleeing from outright catastrophe. The choice was not between starvation and survival but between actuality and opportunity.

Turner and his fellow historians of the frontier have rightly drawn attention to certain social qualities of western life, at least in the non-slave states—its informality, its egalitarianism, its corn-huskings, barn-raisings, and other neighborly practices. But while western settlement was a notable achievement, bringing real as well as hoped-for prosperity to untold thousands of Americans, it was also a source of discontent. The existence of new lands may indirectly have acted as a "safety valve" by providing a release for energies and grievances that in Europe were to lead to so sharp an ideological cleavage between have and have-not. But the lure of the West also acted in the opposite direction. It was apt to raise inordinate hopes and then inevitably to lead to disappointment. It stimulated a permanent, though usually mild, gold-rush mentality which invigorated the alert yet tormented the sluggish and incompetent, since it deprived them of adequate excuse for their failure. "This constant stimulation of hope, emulation, and ambition," wrote the New Englander Thomas Low Nichols, looking back on his boyhood, "often produced . . . feverish effort and discontent. Few were content to live at home and cultivate the niggard soil of New Hampshire." Here is one explanation for the rabid demonologies of American history: the intense suspicion of others, the readiness to identify conspiracies, the hatred of Indians, Negroes, foreign-born immigrants, or anyone else against whom blame may be laid for one's own ill success. Some of these tensions will be considered in chapter vi.

For the moment it is enough to comment briefly on the fact that the West during the period became a distinct force in American affairs. Its geographical and spiritual limits were perpetually changing and never completely separate from those of the East. But its problems were different, at least in degree, from the problems of older-settled areas. Land—title, price, settlement—was a paramount consideration. New preoccupations encouraged a new vocabulary. When Noah Webster was challenged in 1816 for having included the words "locate" and "location" in his dictionary, although they were not in the English dictionaries, he retorted, "no, Sir; and this was one reason why I compiled mine. How can the English *locate* lands, when they have no lands to locate!" And some years after Jackson's era, the lecturer-essayist Ralph Waldo Emerson was to note during a visit to Iowa that men there talked in a settler's idiom: "give me a *quarter-section* of pie," they would say at the dinner table.

The marketing of produce was another matter of acute concern, and hence the western interest in steamboats, highways, canals, and railroads. The availability of credit was a related issue. The prospect for culture in the Mississippi Valley was yet another topic that began to harass the westerner.

This last reflection introduces a corrective to the picture of the West as a zone of transit and upheaval. Most settlers *did* settle, despite the minority of unlucky, unskilful, or unstable men who moved on again and again. Parts of northern Ohio, Indiana, and Illinois soon took on an air of decent accomplishment, with their neat white townships whose New England names bore witness to the origin of their founders. In the early 1800's, for instance, the people of Granville, Massachusetts, decided to move. They selected a site whose "peculiar blending of hill and valley" resembled their old home and established the town of Granville in central Ohio. Their Congregational church—pastor, deacons, and members—was transplanted intact. A compact to regulate the new community was drawn up. One hundred and seventy-six Yankees said good-by to Massachusetts. They journeyed for over six weeks, and on reaching the site of their projected town in Ohio, their first act was to release the oxen from the wagons and listen to a sermon by the pastor. Whole counties were populated by families of New England stock. Other counties a little to the south saw a mingling of pioneers from New England with those from Virginia and North Carolina. Their accents, building styles, farming methods, pattern of education, diet, and other social customs differed a good deal; and a certain amount of mutual hostility resulted. In the southern Middle West, settlers from Virginia and North Carolina preserved their old ways of life with little or no dilution.

Farther south again, in Kentucky, Tennessee, or Mississippi, the planter—as soon as he could spare the time and labor—erected a mansion (sometimes, though not generally, neoclassical in design) which gave an impressive look of permanence to his recently acquired plantation. Roads crisscrossed the land; villages grew at their intersections, or by river ferries. The fortunate village became a town, and some—Cleveland, Cincinnati, Pittsburgh, Lexington, Nashville, Memphis—flourished mightily. Schools, churches, newspapers, colleges, sprang into being—too many colleges, in fact, through the vigorous competition for influence and membership between the major religious sects of an ebullient Protestantism. A traveler on a Mississippi steamboat or a western stagecoach might observe extraordinary, indeed hilarious, incongruities of dress and demeanor among his fellow passengers. But, by and large, the West made itself over with amazing rapidity; it seemed touchingly anxious to supply whatever it still lacked in order to surpass the East in the refinements of civilization.

Moreover, the western vision of expansion was not entirely unlimited. These were not yet the high days of "Manifest Destiny." The travel accounts of Zebulon M. Pike, Henry M. Brackenridge, and the Stephen H. Long expedition, published in 1810, 1817, and 1823, respectively, conveyed the idea that beyond Missouri and Arkansas lay an arid, treeless waste; it was marked on maps as the "Great American Desert" and held unsuitable for occupation by American farmers. "Until our country becomes supercharged with population," said

The West

Brackenridge, "there is scarcely any probability of settlers venturing far into these regions." The Long expedition reinforced his opinion, declaring that the area between the Missouri River and the Rocky or "Stony" Mountains (as they were originally named) would "serve as a barrier to prevent too great an extension of our population westward," as well as a barrier against possible enemies.

This point of view was widely accepted; the expansionist fervor of President Jackson was not shared by most of his countrymen for a decade afterward. Senator Benton of Missouri, for instance, was later to reveal himself a devotee of Manifest Destiny who wished the United States to expand all the way to the Pacific. But in the 1820's and 1830's his ideas were more modest. He urged the full occupation of the Mississippi Valley and the development of a western land route which would open to America the trade of the Orient. But he was convinced that the Rockies marked the natural boundary of the United States and that a new, independent (though friendly) nation would grow up beyond the mountains. Here, in the much-quoted words he uttered in a debate on the future of Oregon (1825), "the western limit of this republic should be drawn, and the statue of the fabled god, Terminus, should be raised upon its highest peak, never to be thrown down."

In large part this attitude rested upon a misconception of the terrain. For two hundred years American settlers had been used to well-wooded country. When they came across a treeless area in Alabama, they avoided it for a number of years, until they realized by degrees that it was a splendidly fertile belt. They hesitated similarly at the edge of the Great Plains, exaggerating the difficulties that confronted them.

There was also a residual uneasiness, inherited from Montesquieu and other eighteenth-century pundits and heightened by current sectional jealousies, at the vast size of the United States. According to Montesquieu, disunion threatened any republic that grew too large: "It is natural to a republic to have only a small territory; otherwise it cannot long subsist." Since his day, communications had been revolutionized by the invention of the steamboat and the railway. In 1832 Samuel F. B. Morse started to experiment with the electric telegraph, on which he filed a preliminary patent in 1837. But neither the telegraph nor the railroad (nor the American road system) was sufficiently developed by 1837 to draw together all parts of the Union. Indeed, it was beginning to seem that no mere physical expedient could create warmer relations between slaveholding South and free-soil North.

Moreover, the western states, once settled, revealed a conservatism akin to that of the East. Initially jubilant at their growing strength, they were not much interested in eastern complaints about loss of population and loss of comparative political power. If Massachusetts, Virginia, and the Carolinas increased in population by only a few per cent from 1820 to 1830, their loss through emigration was the West's gain. Now, however, the prescient westerner could foresee a time when his own section might lose strength in favor of a newer West.

For all these reasons, there was a temporary lull in the westward impulse at the end of the period. This lull did not preclude the continued settlement of Oregon and Texas, or the taking-up of new lands along the frontier. There was no major drawing-in of effort. Both West and East were ambivalent in their approach to the phenomenon of expansion, glorying in the process even while it dismayed them. Western development

The West

was increasingly tinged with sectional jealousy; the antagonism of North and South governed much that was said and done in the new territories and states. Expansion was, too, an epitome of the whole national effort. The economy of the United States had, for the moment, in true American fashion, bitten off at least as much as it could chew.

V

Commerce and Industry

Seventeen eighty-nine was a year of marked prosperity for the United States, 1837 a year in which she entered a severe slump. But the comparison is of course misleading; between these dates the American economy showed an impressive trend from vulnerability and uncertainty to strength and confidence.

The initial uncertainty of 1789—somewhat mitigated by the recovery in trade of the previous two or three years—derived from America's former status and the problem of her future economic position. A group of colonies had left the mercantilist circle of the British Empire. Their role in that system had in some senses been passive and even ignominious. The American colonies were the furnishers of raw materials or the extractive produce of agriculture—timber, tobacco, and the like. In return the colonies absorbed the manufactures of the mother country: a long list of items that embraced everything from salt to snuffboxes, fine furniture to farm implements, cloth to cutlery, engravings to iron bars. The pattern was artificial to the extent that it was a closed circuit whose currents were deliberately directed and restricted. Most varieties of manufacture were forbidden, at any rate in theory, to the Americans. Economically no less than politically they were bound to Britain.

But that is not to say that the colonists were "exploited" or that their economic development was seriously retarded. There were positive benefits to membership in a mercantilist empire. American shipbuilders and merchants in overseas trade thrived under the shelter of the Navigation Acts. The triangles of trade linking the American colonies with the British West Indies, with the slave coast of West Africa, and with the mother country were particularly profitable. American farmers had a West Indian market for their grain, American millers for their flour; molasses from the Caribbean sugar islands could be converted into valuable cargoes of rum and the rum exchanged for Negro slaves; tobacco and naval stores taken into Bristol, Glasgow, or London could be exchanged for the multifarious products of Great Britain. By and large the arrangement worked well in economic terms, since it merely canalized what was at the time a natural balance of economies.

When the United States achieved political independence, her economic freedom was still open to question. Trading connections with Britain continued, but the United States was no longer a prime beneficiary within the sanctuary of the empire. Nor was she automatically admitted to the mercantilist spheres of France and Spain. England hoped partially to replace the United States by Canada in the scheme of things; English shipowners looked forward to a period of ease when they would no longer face the competition of the colonial merchant marine; and some English pamphleteers wrote of the United States as an Adam of political economy shut out from Eden.

In 1789 this vision of limbo remained to be dispelled. That it was no more than a somber vision was, however, already apparent to shrewd eyes. For the ties of mercantilism were substituted the equally effective ties of economic necessity—a necessity felt on both sides of the Atlantic. Throughout the next half-century, well over 50 per cent of America's foreign trade was with Britain or British possessions. With some exceptions, the old routes of ocean-borne commerce stayed open, and new ones were pioneered.

As was suggested in chapter iii, the European wars of 1793–1815 were of salient importance in promoting America's foreign commerce. Her ships and her products were eagerly sought by both sides, and where official prohibitions existed they were evaded by smuggling or by liberal interpretations of the law. American ships found their way, and met a welcome, in the harbors of the French West Indies, of Spanish colonies in the New World, and even—despite British governmental reluctance—of the British West Indies, where Jay's Treaty had failed to secure a satisfactory entry. So vigorous and so essential was this traffic that it persisted during the War of 1812 as it had done, clandestinely, during the years of Jefferson and Madison's experiments at embargo and non-intercourse.

American vessels pioneered fresh lines of trade in other corners of the globe. Soon after the British link was broken, they appeared for the first time in the Mediterranean and the Baltic, in Latin America and the Far East. Technically the "East India" trade was under the mercantilist regulation of the colonial powers—Britain, France, Spain, and the Netherlands—where it was not within the frigidly antiforeign domain of China. But in actuality the colonial powers permitted American ships to share in the abundant commerce of the Orient, and China put American merchants on the same footing as those of Europe who came to chaffer at its one port of outlet, Canton. From Canton the American brought home tea, chinaware, silks, and "nankeens," paying for them with the furs of seals and otters collected in the Falkland Isles and the Pacific Northwest, or with more fragrant cargoes such as sandalwood from Hawaii or opium acquired in Turkey. A high proportion of these American vessels were built and manned by New Englanders, who likewise roamed the world on whaling expeditions. In the words of an Independence Day address by Timothy Flint at Leominster, Massachusetts, in 1815, "Commerce soon raised the American stars over a thousand vessels. The Arab, the Hindoo, the Chinese, the inhabitants of the isles, of the equator, and the frozen zone, conversed and trafficked with the muscular, enterprizing and calculating sons of New-England, and for the first time learned, that a great empire had sprung up . . . in a country but recently rescued from the wilderness."

At the end of the Napoleonic Wars the American merchant marine flourished still more. The technology of shipbuilding had a long heritage in the United States. Timber was still plentiful, hemp was inexpensive, and the small vessels of the day could be constructed in any of dozens of little inlets along the coast. The craft launched from these slipways were sturdy, well designed, and cheaper than those of Britain. The crews that manned them, especially in the earlier part of the century, were often skilled seamen, and their mates and captains were usually men of exceptional toughness and intelligence. Some shipowners grew opulent. Stephen Girard of Philadelphia, who at his death in 1831 left nine million dollars, first established himself as a shipper, though his subsequent accumulation of wealth came from banking. Israel Thorndike of Boston, reputedly the richest man in New England when he died in 1832, amassed over two million dollars through overseas trade.

The organization of foreign commerce gradually changed. While the minor ports of Maine or Massachusetts went on building ships and trading to the best of their ability, the major commercial activity became increasingly concentrated in a few large ports—Boston, New York, Philadelphia, Baltimore, New Orleans. In 1790 Philadelphia was the largest city in the United States, with a population of 42,000 as against New York's 33,000. After them, considerably smaller, came Boston, Charleston, and Baltimore. Thirty years later, New York had ousted Philadelphia from first place (124,000 against 113,000); Baltimore was third with 63,000 inhabitants, followed by Boston (43,000) and New Orleans (27,000), with Charleston in sixth place. All of the first five went on growing at an impressive rate; those on the Atlantic coast competed strenuously with one another. But each year New York crept farther and farther ahead of its rivals in population, wealth, and financial dominance.

One stage in the process was the establishment in 1818 of a transatlantic packet line by venturesome New York merchants. Hitherto, ships had sailed at irregular intervals, when their cargoes were complete. The "Black Ball" packets left New York for Liverpool (a British port whose rapid rise paralleled that of New York) on a regular, advertised schedule, with great convenience to merchants and travelers alike. Under the vagaries of sail the date of arrival could be only roughly predicted. But at this stage in ocean commerce any attempt at a reliable schedule was welcome. Thanks to minor improvements in design, the time required for the crossing was reduced by an average of two or three days between 1818 and 1837. By the latter date the Liverpool or New York merchant had a choice of two or more "liner" sailings each week. As pilotage, brokerage, warehousing, and other port facilities were developed, New York strengthened its claim to be the nation's commercial capital. In through the jaws of New York's capacious harbor—and, to a lesser extent, those of other ports—flowed the woolen and cotton manufactures that made up a quarter of America's imports (in value) during the decades after the War of 1812: the sugar, coffee, and other commodities that the nation could not produce for itself. Out through New York passed many of the products that America exported.

For most of the period, raw cotton was the principal export. It was so unimportant a crop—in comparison with tobacco—in 1794 that John Jay, negotiating his treaty in London, seems not to have realized that it had any appreciable part to play in the American economy. By 1837, however, the national production of cotton was in the region of a million bales a year and still increasing rapidly. The proportion of this output devoted to export had a cash value of over $300 million and accounted for more than 40 per cent of America's total exports. By that time tobacco, while still a significant export, made up only about 10 per cent of the export total; cotton had driven it from first place as far back as 1803. Much of this annual mountain of cotton was shipped from New Orleans. But a considerable quantity—so widespread was the entrepôt activity of New York—was transshipped through the northern port or disposed of there through Anglo-American credit houses and banking firms even if it did not physically travel via New York.

Other export commodities, such as wheat and flour, beef and pork, bore testimony to the expansion of western territory and domestic commerce outlined in the previous chapter. The initial settlement of the West and its subsequent economic development both depended upon communications: in other words, on what came to be known as "internal improvements." Land and communication were twin American preoccupations for much of the nineteenth century; the enhancement of the one intimately affected the other. Something has already been said of the turnpikes and other road systems that began to crawl across the map as soon as American independence was attained. They were far from constituting a comprehensive network. Most of them were local ventures, running between two towns or across the watershed between two river routes. Only one major, paved, national highway was undertaken—the "National Road" from Cumberland on the upper Potomac through the Alleghenies to Wheeling (now in West Virginia) on the east bank of the Ohio. This section was finished in 1818. Fifteen years later the National Road, financed by successive federal appropriations, had got as far west as Columbus, Ohio. Some maps of the 1830's show the road continuing on through Indianapolis and Terre Haute to St. Louis on the Mississippi. This extension was never completed under federal auspices. However, the National Road was much traveled. Another highway linked its eastern terminus with Baltimore and the seaboard; a route from Philadelphia to Pittsburgh also had a connection with Wheeling; an alternative western route from Wheeling passed through Lexington and Shawneetown to the Mississippi; and from Columbus a trail ran on to Cincinnati and Louisville.

This was one of several linked "systems," though they grew up piecemeal without systematic planning. Settlers moved in along the roads in one direction, while their produce moved back in the opposite direction. The proliferation of highways and the feverish competition between the eastern states and cities that promoted them had a marked effect in forcing down the cost of road transportation.

Nevertheless, freight charges remained far higher by land routes than by water, in fact prohibitively high for agricultural and other products whose value was low in proportion to weight. Just after the War of 1812, for example, wagon drivers were charging thirteen dollars to carry a single barrel of flour from Pittsburgh to Philadelphia. As a result, especially for the movement of freight, highways were of second importance to waterways. It is no accident that the western towns whose populations increased most rapidly were also inland ports. Their rise was a function of the vigorous growth of commerce on the Great Lakes, on the Mississippi and its tributaries (particularly the Ohio), and indeed on all the larger American rivers up to the limit of navigation. A wonderfully varied procession of flatboats, rafts, and barges glided down the Ohio and the Mississippi. Some of the men who steered them were professionals, like the semimythical Mike Fink, "king of the keelboatmen," who died in the 1820's. Some were settlers on the way to new homes. Some were casual laborers like young Abraham Lincoln of Illinois, who twice joined a flatboat crew on a voyage to New Orleans.

One serious objection to river travel was the strength of the current. A boat could not make more than about ten miles a day upstream, even by dint of laborious exertion. In many cases it was simpler to break up the boat at the end of its downstream journey and sell the timber. But that did not solve the problem of developing a two-way traffic. The solution came with the steamboat. European and American inventors had been experimenting with the idea for over twenty years when Robert Fulton constructed his *Clermont* in 1807. Equipped with paddle wheels and a Boulton and Watt low-pressure steam engine imported from England, the *Clermont* chugged upriver without trouble from New York to Albany, a distance of 150 miles, at an average speed of five miles per hour. After this demonstration of the feasibility of steamboat travel as a source of profit, inventor-mechanics and entrepreneurs such as Fulton, John Stevens, Robert R. Livingston, Aaron Ogden, and Nicholas J. Roosevelt became associated in intricate combinations and rivalries, as they strove to improve the performance of their vessels and to secure monopolies over the highly profitable estuary traffic of the Hudson, Delaware, and Chesapeake. Their efforts at monopoly eventually failed, in part because of the Supreme Court ruling in the case of *Gibbons* v. *Ogden* (1824), which in effect threw the arena open to all entrepreneurial gladiators with the capital and courage to enter it. By 1837 no large town on the eastern seaboard, including those that lay far upriver, was without its ferry and other steamboat services.

The innovation did not take long to appear on the western waters. In 1811 the first western steamboat was built and launched at Pittsburgh, under the auspices of Nicholas J. Roosevelt. It succeeded in reaching New Orleans. The vessel cost him nearly $40,000; profits on the Mississippi were never so high as those in the East; and there was a pause before his initiative was widely followed. However, within ten or fifteen years the steamboat was a familiar sight throughout the main arteries of the Mississippi, thronging the wharves of New Orleans and bringing wealth and population to a score of river towns. One source of their prosperity was shipbuilding. The evolution of the high-pressure engine added much to the speed and utility of the ubiquitous steamboat with its giant paddle wheels, gaunt smokestacks, and ornate decks. It was a distinctively American creation that never failed to impress the European visitor. Or to alarm him: the accident rate was high, even with a four-foot draft, on rivers that were full of snags and sandbars. Despite its flamboyant aspects, however, the steamboat was an economic fact of vital significance. The steamboat tonnage on western waters was by 1837 roughly equal to that of all the steamships in the British merchant navy.

Yet, in addition to their navigational hazards, the rivers of the United States had obvious disadvantages. They formed a series of separate systems, and they flowed in the wrong direction, so far as the paths of commerce were concerned. The remedy was to construct artificial waterways. By this means the water routes of the eastern seaboard could be extended through the Appalachians, to connect with the Ohio and its tributaries, and the Great Lakes could also be brought into service so as to join East to West and North to South.

Some canals had been projected even before 1789. George Washington was a pioneer advocate of improved navigation on the Potomac and James rivers, in order to bind the trans-Allegheny hinterland to Virginia. But his and most of the other early endeavors were modest in scale, comprising not much more than a few miles of canal to bypass rapids on existing rivers. The first and most sensationally profitable major scheme, argued for almost a generation before it came into being under the tireless leadership of Governor DeWitt Clinton, was New York's Erie Canal. A "big ditch" 363 miles long, it must be ranked—with the packet lines and the natural magnificence of Manhattan's situation—as one of the three principal factors in the supremacy won by New York City over its seaport competitors. In the first year of operation, 1825, the Erie Canal collected more than a million dollars in tolls—one-seventh of the original outlay—from the thirteen thousand boats and rafts that moved along it between Buffalo and Albany. Goods that had cost a hundred dollars a ton to haul between those towns by wagon could now go by water for a tenth of the expense. The Northwest had acquired a splendid outlet for its products, and New York an immense new market for native or imported manufactures. Accessibility acted like magic.

The results were not lost upon the eastern states and cities. New York had already constructed a Champlain canal at the same time as the Erie route, to link the Hudson with the St. Lawrence. It hastened to encourage subsidiary, "feeder" canals which would widen the Erie trade domain. Spurred into action, citizens of Boston laid plans for a canal across Massachusetts to Albany, in the hope of challenging New York's capture of western commerce. As it happened, the scheme was never carried out. But the aggressive entrepreneurs of Philadelphia rushed into the fray. Within a year of the completion of the Erie Canal, they had persuaded their own state to undertake a road-and-canal route from their city inland to Pittsburgh. The difficulties were formidable, since no convenient valley such as the Mohawk pierced the high Allegheny wall west of

Philadelphia. Still, the prize was considerable. At this stage, before navigation on the Great Lakes had been improved, Pennsylvania had easier access than New York to the western centers of population, and there seemed no reason why Philadelphia's enterprise should not enable it to carry off the palm. The Pittsburgh canal was completed—a remarkable technical achievement which attracted much comment and a good deal of traffic. But rates were higher than on the Erie route; no other eastern canal venture came anywhere near to repeating the success of Erie; and in any case canals began gradually to yield to the railroad. Waterways, even where artificial, froze up for part of the year in the northern states, and canals were obliged to conform to some extent to the lay of the land.

The railroad, on the other hand, could operate all the year around; it was much less the victim of the terrain; and, though the early tracks and engines were subject to many limitations, it held out the promise of extremely rapid transit. These considerations led the Pennsylvania promoters to incorporate a railroad in their Pittsburgh route, stimulated the New Yorkers to construct an Albany-Buffalo railroad parallel to the Erie, and induced the bold yet prudent capitalists of Massachusetts to build not a canal but a railroad across their state from Boston to Albany. It was a confused situation, in which for twenty years after the advent of the railroad in America (during the late 1820's) enterprise hesitated between it and the construction of waterways. This uncertainty is epitomized in the name of a company—the South Carolina Canal and Railroad—chartered in 1828, and in two other simultaneous activities of that year. At Washington, on July 4, President Adams dug the first spadeful of soil to initiate the Chesapeake and Ohio Canal (a descendant of George Washington's Potomac schemes).

The Nation Takes Shape

On the same national holiday a ceremony was held in Baltimore to mark the beginning of the Baltimore and Ohio Railroad, which in point of time was the first iron road to reach into the interior from the seaboard.

Others quickly followed. By 1833 a line was open from Charleston, South Carolina, that extended for over 130 miles—the longest in the world at the moment of its inauguration. In 1835 a 42-mile railroad was completed from Boston to Worcester, Massachusetts. Another, the Western Railroad, was already chartered to extend this line across the state to the border with New York, where it would meet one from Albany. To the loyal citizens of Massachusetts, the "Western" Railroad meant everything that its name could imply. As one of them, Edward Everett, proclaimed at a railroad promotional meeting in Boston, in 1835, "The country, by nature or art, is traversed, crossed, reticulated, (pardon me, sir, this long word; the old ones are too short to describe these prodigious works,) with canals and railroads, rivers and lakes. The entire west is moving to meet us; by water, land, and stream, they ride, they sail, they drive, they paddle, they whiz,—they do all but fly down towards us."

Should "good old Massachusetts" permit this peaceful western invasion, "bringing the fruits of their industry, and taking ours in return"? Everett had no doubts on the score. Nor had his audience. Nor, indeed, had any of the eastern coastal states. Nor, for that matter, had the western states themselves, although their resources in population and money were naturally inferior. The first constitution of Missouri—applying for statehood in 1820—declared that "internal improvements shall forever be encouraged by the government of this State, and it shall be the duty of the general assembly, as soon as may be, to make provision by law for ascertaining the most popular objects of improvement, in relation both to roads and navigable waters." Similar clauses were inserted in the new constitutions of Michigan (1835) and Arkansas (1836). State action went much further than mere exhortation.

Federal policy was, by comparison, hesitant and indecisive. Both President Jefferson and, more firmly, his Treasury Secretary Albert Gallatin, favored the application of public funds to internal improvements. Jefferson suggested in his second inaugural address (1805) that once the bulk of the national debt had been discharged, "the revenue thereby liberated, may . . . be supplied, in time of peace, to rivers, canals, roads, arts, manufactures, education, and other great objects within each state." However, he also felt that such programs were not sanctioned by the Constitution and ought not to be undertaken until an amendment had been ratified which would permit federal support of internal improvements. In 1808 Gallatin drew up an ambitious scheme for a ten-year program of road and canal construction for which $20 million would be provided by the federal government. Though Jefferson included the plan in his annual message to Congress, the program was never implemented.

The National Road, already mentioned, was the first fruit of federal enterprise in internal improvement. There were few other fruits. Neither Madison nor Monroe was enthusiastic about such federal initiative. In 1822 Monroe vetoed a bill providing funds for the repair of the road, out of constitutional scruple. Work on it was suspended until 1825, when federal money was again available for extensions. In that year John Quincy Adams became President. Like Gallatin, he was keenly interested in developing a bold yet orderly national system of roads and canals. He recommended the course in his inaugural address and continued to press the idea during his four years in office. Under his administration more than $2 million were appropriated for roads and harbors, as against a total of about $1 million appropriated for the same purposes during all the administrations of his predecessors. There were throughout the period minor federal activities by way of surveys, building of lighthouses, dredging of rivers and harbors, and so on. But nothing of major significance was done. Adams' larger proposals were ignored or derided, to his bitter regret. Despite a national income from land sales and (more substantially) from import duties so big that in 1826 a Senate committee actually bewailed the "serious inconvenience of an overflowing Treasury," despite the feasibility of Gallatin's and Adams' projects and the eloquence of such western spokesmen as Henry Clay who welcomed federal aid to develop communications, despite all their efforts, the federal government played only a small part in the "reticulation" that Everett referred to. After Adams, Andrew Jackson reverted to the strict constructionism of the old-style Republicans. Vetoing (1830) a bill to authorize government expenditure on the Maysville turnpike in Kentucky, he subsequently showed his disapproval by terminating various federal road and canal grants.

The strict-constructionist view is not easy to comprehend at this distance in time. However, there were perfectly understandable if not always edifying grounds for objecting to federal intervention. It was extremely difficult to apportion funds to the individual states on any equitable basis. Again, any plan for internal improvement was bedeviled by local and sectional rivalries from which it was perhaps better for the national government to remain aloof. Third, granted that the "reticulation" remained a patchwork, with wasteful duplication of effort and an irritating assortment of railroad gauges, it cannot be said that the general progress of internal improvement—in communications at any rate—was greatly hampered by federal indifference. If Gallatin's and Adams' plans had been adopted, development might have been tidier. It could hardly have been quicker. A surprising quantity of capital was forthcoming, much of it subscribed by European and particularly British investors. But impressive sums were furnished by native American effort, in part as a consequence of extremely low federal taxation. In the South, where too much capital was locked up in slaveholding (and where there were some long, deep rivers whose fall line was far inland), the progress of roads, canals, and railways was not so astonishing. Elsewhere, since Americans were predisposed toward investment in land and in internal improvements—the two great areas of speculative enterprise in the United States of the early nineteenth century—there seemed no limit to the number or grandiosity of schemes that might be set in motion.

Moreover, if the federal government stood aside, individual state governments did not hesitate to direct the economies of their commonwealths. They chartered banks and corporations on quite specific terms. They entered commerce and industry through the device of the mixed corporation, by which state funds were allotted for enterprises intrusted to chartered organizations. They undertook public works programs: the Philadelphia-Pittsburgh "main line" canal is an example of such an operation in Pennsylvania. In short, the era can hardly be understood as one of unqualified laissez-faire capitalism—though of course state governments and business corporations were by no means remote from one another. On the contrary, ties were very close. There was an identity of actual personnel. And there was an identity of interest, both in terms of interstate rivalry and of the larger context of development. A work such as *Mitchell's Compendium of the Internal Improvements of the United States* (1835) breathes the excited spirit of the age. "Projects," it says, "which a few years ago would have seemed visionary and chimerical, have been carried into execution, with results outstripping the most sanguine calculations; immense expenditures of capital have been made, and investments still more enormous are calculated throughout every part of the Union. . . . It has been discovered," the author goes on, "that works of internal improvement, if wisely executed, enrich, instead of impoverishing a country."

S. A. Mitchell's general assertion is accurate enough. Between 1820 and 1838 eighteen states authorized credit advances of $60 million for canals, $43 million for railroads, $4.5 million for turnpikes, and subscribed $52.5 million for bank stocks. Pennsylvania was the largest borrower, New York second. Mitchell's qualification, "if wisely executed," was also sound. In the boom psychology of the 1830's such cautions were brushed aside. The result, starting in 1837, was a recession so sharp that scores of projects, not to mention the banks and monetary devices on which they rested, suddenly began to appear visionary and chimerical again. The states, and individual Americans, had overreached themselves. At the end of Jackson's second administration the national scene was temporarily darkened.

The degree of reality attached to money varies according to the condition of the economy. In Jacksonian America, during the boom in land investment and internal improvements, it is not much too wild an exaggeration to say that money was—in some situations—no object. The currency's standard was hope. Thus, investment in western city development or along the routes of new canals and railroads promised dazzling profits. A hundred putative metropolises came to nothing, or nothing much. But those that did—Buffalo, Cleveland, Cincinnati, Toledo, Chicago—offered fantastic returns to the lucky few. A man who happened to buy land on the site of what became Chicago could get it in the 1820's for the usual $1.25 an acre. By 1832 the price was quoted at $100, and a couple of years later it rocketed to $3,500.

This was exceptional, however; and not long after that, money became a more real and depressingly scarce commodity in the United States. In some portions of the economy, especially manufacturing, it had long presented itself in this sober guise. True, there was some manufacturing and heavy industry at the outset of the period. Coal, lead, and copper were mined in several areas. There was a quantity of ironworks. The level of technical ability was fairly high in New England and in some of the middle states. In Lynn, Massachusetts, and some other Yankee towns shoemaking was an advanced art. Woolen clothing was spun and woven, particularly in New England, with some proficiency as a domestic manufacture. In 1788 the first factory to produce woolen cloth was opened at Hartford, Connecticut. It provided the material for the suit worn by President Washington at his inauguration in 1789. Two years later, the New Jersey legislature incorporated "The Society for Establishing Useful Manufactures." Much commended by Alexander Hamilton, who in the same year submitted a powerful report on the subject of manfactures to Congress, the New Jersey society had ambitious plans. For instance, it bought a mill site by the Passaic falls, at what became the industrial

town of Paterson. In 1832 the New Yorker Philip Hone recorded in his diary a visit to these falls. The spectacle was
enjoyable; however, Paterson was a "cotton spinning dirty
village. . . . . Green trees have given place to brown stone
walls, and the singing of birds to the everlasting noise of
spinning jennies and power looms."

But it will be noted that Hone's trip took place forty years
after the establishment of the "S.U.M." For those who had
the cause of manufacturing at heart, they were years of
achievement considerably tempered by disappointment. The
woolen factory at Hartford failed; so did the New Jersey
venture; and Hamilton's report persuaded only those who
were persuaded already. As he himself admitted, the "objections to the pursuit of manufactures in the United States"
appeared to be threefold—"scarcity of hands, dearness of labor,
want of capital"—of which he conceded that the first two were
serious difficulties. There was a dearth of skilled workmen, and
especially of capable foremen and factory managers. Because
of the prosperity of the country and the mobility of its population, wages were high, and it was extremely hard to train
and keep a stable working force. And the lack of capital was
an important disadvantage. Both European and American investors thought they had better uses for their capital than to
sink it in American manufactures. There was no reason for
British capitalists to encourage the growth of industrialism in
the United States; until 1824 Britain theoretically prohibited
the emigration of skilled artisans and from the same motives
might not wish capital to emigrate for manufacturing purposes. In the commercial centers of the United States, where
many made a livelihood from foreign trade, there seemed little
point in seeking to challenge the supremacy of European

manufactures. Investment in shipping and commerce was obviously wise. Investment in land and in internal improvements was of equal utility.

But manufactures? To Hamilton's list of disadvantages could be added the American lack of machinery and of the knowledge of how to construct and maintain it. All the major mechanical inventions of the period were European. The level of technological ability in the United States seemed irreparably lower. Moreover, there was a widespread American feeling that manufacturing would be positively harmful. It would lead to the growth of cities, of an urban poor; it would (so Jefferson and his associates maintained) corrupt America's ideal of an agrarian democracy. This feeling persisted throughout the period, though in diminishing strength. It is exemplified in the reaction of American visitors to England, which was easily the foremost industrial nation of the world. "At this stage of our population," wrote Joshua E. White, a Savannah cotton dealer who traveled there in 1810, "it is maddening folly and stupid policy to aim at a rivalship with Great Britain in her manufactures; and from the moment we see such places as Manchester and Birmingham in our country, should we date the commencement of a system . . . fraught with principles most inimical to the happiness of the people." Joseph Ballard, a Boston merchant who toured England in 1815, was appalled by the poverty and injustice that seemed to be engendered by the factory system. He thought that in Sheffield, by a savage irony of industrialism, "the poorer classes are worse off for the articles which they immediately manufacture than the inhabitants of the American back settlements are." Even an American manufacturer, Zachariah Allen of Rhode Island, who visited England in 1825, was as much depressed by the grimness of cities like Liverpool and Manchester as impressed by their progress in the "useful arts."

There was, then, a marked American reluctance to attempt to emulate Britain—in part from a conviction that the task was economically impossible, in part from a belief that it was morally and socially undesirable. Expressed in different form, it took the shape of what by 1790 was already an American national cliché, namely, a stress upon the primacy of agriculture. The husbandman came first, not merely as a matter of chronology, not simply as an economic fact, but as an American moral judgment or shibboleth. Jefferson was one of countless writers and orators who sang the praises of the American farmer and valued his product over that of all other artisans. Advocates of manufacturing, such as Hamilton in 1791 or Henry Clay in 1824, had to reckon with the situation and pay lip service to the tradition. Thus Clay, arguing vehemently in favor of American manufactures under a protective tariff, nevertheless conceded that his countrymen would always be "an agricultural people."

No wonder that the early ventures at Hartford and Paterson were abortive. Yet within a generation the atmosphere changed appreciably. The prolonged European wars of 1793–1815 had their effect. Although their first result was to stimulate American maritime enterprise, the Jeffersonian boycott of foreign trade instead stimulated American manufactures. The blockade of the War of 1812 increased the tendency. In the next fifteen years, as New England gradually became the stronghold of American manufacturing, so the Yankee merchant and shipowner became converted to factory enterprise. The shift is mirrored in the long congressional struggle over tariff policy. While New England remained predominantly mercantile, its seaport communities fought for low tariffs on foreign imports. Daniel Webster, their great champion in Congress, thundered against the iniquities of the tariffs of 1816 and 1824. But as the balance swung, so did the direction of Webster's oratorical artillery. Though his Massachusetts colleague in the Senate disagreed with him in 1828, Webster voted in favor of the severely protectionist tariff of that year. In 1830 the trend was further dramatized when, in a congressional election at Boston, the merchant and free-trade propagandist Henry Lee was soundly beaten by the manufacturer and tariff propagandist Nathan Appleton.

In short, entrepreneurs were emerging in significant numbers. Hamilton's ideas had been shared by many of the leading men of commerce in the East, who little by little became linked in entrepreneurial alliances. Hamilton himself, as the son-in-law of Philip Schuyler, was associated with some of the most powerful clans of New York. Such men, and their counterparts in Boston, Baltimore, or Philadelphia, lent active or tacit support to the whole Hamiltonian financial program: for a funded debt, a national bank, a properly regulated currency, a tariff structure. When it suited them, these men turned their talents and their capital into manufacturing. This is the story of the Browns of Providence, Rhode Island, for example, and the Lowells of Boston.

There was a chronic lack of mechanical equipment and mechanical skill in Hamilton's America; there was also—as events soon proved—a reservoir of national ingenuity. Americans adapted themselves quickly. If the fundamental inventions were European, the improvements and modifications were often contributed by Americans. Shortage of labor, skilled or otherwise, provided a strong incentive for using machinery to make good the deficiency. Although the steam engine came from England, improvements owed much to the resourceful Oliver Evans, who began to build high-pressure engines in Pennsylvania in the first decade of the century. By the end of the period other inventor-mechanics in Philadelphia were constructing and even exporting steam locomotives.

The idea of interchangeable parts, which revolutionized the manufacture of small arms and later of clocks, locks, and other light industry, seems to have originated in France. But it was Eli Whitney, already celebrated for his invention of the cotton gin, who made the notion lucrative. His success, and that of other American enterprise in general, is epitomized in the description by Timothy Dwight of Whitney's factory at New Haven, Connecticut, in 1803:

> This establishment was undertaken by Mr. Whitney without the least experience in manufacturing fire-arms. All his workmen, also, . . . were absolutely unskilled in the business. . . . In these circumstances Mr. Whitney was constrained to adopt methods of his own, and . . . to devise a system in which the more exact operations of his machinery might supply the want of experience in the workmen.

In the New England textile industry, too, the Browns and Lowells were heavily indebted to clever artisans such as Ozias Wilkinson of Pawtucket, Rhode Island, or David Anthony and his cousins the Wheelers, of Fall River, Massachusetts, who in their turn became wealthy entrepreneurs within a generation.

A further cause of success, particularly in the New England textile industry, lay in the contribution made by immigrant workmen. Hamilton's report on manufactures stressed the benefits that would accrue to America from absorbing skilled European labor. Even before he submitted his report, the observation was confirmed in the figure of Samuel Slater, a talented operative from the Lancashire cotton industry. As in Britain, so in America—on a far smaller scale—it was in the manufacture and especially the spinning of cotton that the application of machinery and factory techniques was most triumphantly demonstrated. Slater, evading the British rules that would have prevented his emigration, came to the United States in 1789. Within a couple of years, putting into use the precious knowledge of spinning processes that he had acquired in England, Slater was managing a small mill at Pawtucket, under the auspices of Moses Brown. The experiment flourished and was soon imitated at other sites in Rhode Island and Massachusetts where water power was available (the application of the steam engine was a later development). The first cotton mill at Fall River opened in 1813.

About the same period Francis Cabot Lowell, who had watched British textile machinery in operation, came home and installed a power loom in an old paper mill at Waltham near Boston. In conjunction with the Jacksons and Appletons, the Lowell family quickly extended its cotton empire through the Merrimack Manufacturing Company (1822) and other corporations. At the falls on the Merrimack River a textile town was built, and named "Lowell" in honor of Francis Cabot Lowell. The Merrimack Company, sometimes in association with other groups of capitalists, subsequently opened mills at a number of falls in New England and elsewhere. It was not only Paterson that became "a cotton spinning dirty village"; the same spectacle was visible at Taunton in Massachusetts, Manchester in New Hampshire, Saco in Maine. The cotton-mill products of New England, valued in 1820 at $2.5 million, increased in a decade to over $15 million.

The Nation Takes Shape

The woolen products of New England increased in the same period from less than $1 million to over $11 million, though cottage industry accounted for a high proportion of this total. Manufacturing developed in other ways, and in other areas than New England, as industrialization began to affect more and more branches of the economy. Ironworks multiplied, and important new techniques were introduced. Pittsburgh began to emerge as a major United States center of iron-founding. The anthracite and bituminous coal resources of Pennsylvania were exploited with growing interest after 1825. Lead-mining gave a new prominence to parts of Missouri, Wisconsin, and Illinois.

In the half-century from 1789 to 1837 the commerce and industry of the United States were undergoing a profound transformation, even if the business depression of the latter year was to halt progress for a short while. The merchant marine was thriving; the craze for internal improvements had wrought marvels; and manufacturing had got off to a good start despite initial disappointments.

In the perspective of world-wide economic development, the American achievement was still dwarfed by that of Europe, especially of Britain. There was a heavy reliance upon Europe for capital, skilled labor, and technological innovation, not to mention a large variety of manufactures that the United States either could not yet produce for herself or preferred in European versions: the list included everything from fine Yorkshire woolen goods and French silks to iron rails for railroad construction. Britain, "this modern Babylon" in the words of one half-awed, half-horrified American visitor, showed no signs of yielding her commercial and industrial supremacy to the infant economy of the United States. Britain

Commerce and Industry

was soon to score over the American merchant marine through the introduction of iron-built steamships which were far beyond the capacity of American yards. New England's textile towns were modest, almost placid communities—Lowell in particular was a showplace—in comparison with the roaring, smoky cities of the Old World. Nor were the new ideas in commerce confined to America. Ready-made clothing, for example, was imported from Europe in the 1830's. And as early as 1819 John Griscom, an American in London, was fascinated by an emporium known as the Soho Bazaar, which seems to have anticipated the American department store by forty years. It was "an exclusive suite of rooms on two floors . . . in which are collected almost every kind of article. . . . This is a new kind of establishment, of which there are, at present, but two in London. The term, as well as the plan, has been imported from India."

The full effects of the Industrial Revolution were still not apparent in the United States by 1837. It was, in truth no less than in congressional rhetoric, a nation still largely devoted to agriculture and territorial expansion. The railroad had not yet replaced canal, river, and turnpike as the main channel of energy and investment in communications. In some respects —for instance, in its banking system—America's was a primitive economy. Much in the way of commerce and industry was localized; the typical internal pattern, with a few significant exceptions, was of small enterprises serving regional markets. But the American economy, though immature, had all the vigor of youth. Despite the panic of 1837, there was no doubt that the graphs of its future activity would continue to rise.

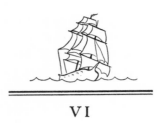

VI

Nationalism and Sectionalism

In the view of Henry Adams, whose study of the administrations of Jefferson and Madison led him to publish a nine-volume survey of that sixteen-year epoch, "the scientific interest of American history centred in national character, and in the workings of a society destined to become vast, in which individuals were important chiefly as types." Since he wrote, seventy years ago, we have become less impressed by "scientific" theories of history. However, his massive analysis is still unsurpassed as a guide to the early years of the nineteenth century. The reasons seem to be that, coupled with a polished, ironical style and a capacity for sustained research, Adams had a tireless curiosity about larger themes, and that two of the themes on which he dwelt with special persistence—nationality and democracy—were indeed as fundamental as he thought. The making of the American nation is accordingly the subject of the present chapter, and the next, chapter vii, is concerned with American democracy.

The evolution of American national feeling is nicely illustrated in a small, unofficial ceremony that took place at Göttingen in Germany. The date was July 4, 1820, and the participants were two American students, of whom one was the Boston historian-to-be George Bancroft. John Adams wrote to his wife in 1776 that July 2, when independence was actually agreed upon by Congress, was the *"Day of Deliverance"* that ought to be celebrated by succeeding generations as "the great anniversary festival." However, within a few years July 4 was singled out as *the* great day on which to commemorate America's national origins. By 1789 it was already a sacred point in the American calendar, to be marked with firecrackers, militia parades, dinners, recitals of the Declaration of Independence, and formal speechmaking.

In their German exile Bancroft and his companion were therefore very much in tradition. No American was more fervently and consciously patriotic than Bancroft, who was to narrate the story of his country's birth in ten proudly lyrical volumes. He more than any other American scholar during the first half of the nineteenth century strove to impress upon his readers the meaning and mission of the United States as a phenomenon without parallel in history.

Several of the symbols of the national spirit he later labored to inculcate are displayed in Bancroft's Göttingen "banquet." They are enumerated for us in the toasts to which the young men raised their glasses. The list included "the sweet nymph Liberty," the heroes of the Revolution, the flag, the American eagle, the Constitution, "the memory of Washington," and "the literary prospects of America." Each is worthy of comment.

"Liberty" is one of those words that have become faceless through overuse, like a coin handled and handled until its insignia are worn away. But to Bancroft and his fellow Americans it was still in 1820 one of the strongly emotive words in the American tongue, which together with "freedom," "union," and others quickened the pulse when they were spoken. Crowded with association, incantatory, they conveyed more in the first thirty years of American independence than, say, "democracy." They struck deep, so deep that when Daniel Webster employed them in a famous speech of 1830, his "LIBERTY AND UNION—NOW AND FOREVER—ONE AND INSEPARABLE" was treated not just as compelling oratory but as great literature, as holy writ.

The practical accomplishment of liberty was the work of the "heroes of the Revolution." Washington, naturally, was foremost. Yet there was no lack of other figures and of moving incidents to awaken the pride of Americans and to fill out the pages of their children's textbooks. A Revolutionary veteran, a little more wrinkled and a little more vague and grandiloquent in his recollections as each year went by, was an indispensable exhibit in Independence Day processions. On one such occasion at Indianapolis in 1822 it turned out that the old soldier in question, though he had undoubtedly fought in the Revolution, had done so as a Hessian on the British side. The embarrassing discovery was overlooked in the mellowness of the moment and in consideration of the fact that he had after all remained behind at the end of the war to become a good American. This story may be apocryphal, since the incident has also been ascribed to other dates and places. However, it has an element of poetic truth. The authentic veteran could tell stirring anecdotes of the discomfiture of the British redcoats at Lexington and Concord, of the audacious descent on Quebec by Montgomery and Benedict

Arnold, the exploits of Ethan Allen at Ticonderoga and of George Rogers Clark at Vincennes, the misery at Valley Forge, the bloody onslaught of Mad Anthony Wayne at Stony Point, the British surrenders at Saratoga and Yorktown.

Cherished slogans entered the national heritage from the war—Israel Putnam's "Don't fire until you see the whites of their eyes," John Paul Jones's "I have not yet begun to fight." Articles of national faith were consecrated by the war. One was that Americans, having defeated the strongest nation in the world, were therefore by tournament rules the champions in valor and military ability. As the British minister to the United States, Robert Liston, wrote home in 1799, Americans had such an "overweening idea of American Prowess and American Talents that they do not scruple to talk of the United States as an overmatch for any nation in Europe." Another article of faith concerned the superiority of the American volunteer fighting man to the professional. If the Massachusetts minutemen and militia could give so good an account of themselves against trained European troops at Concord and Bunker Hill, or the farmers of Vermont against Burgoyne's men at Bennington, or the southerners under Morgan against Tarleton at Cowpens, then America possessed an invincible civilian army which she could summon from the plow at a few days' notice and disband with equal simplicity.

The flag that Bancroft toasted was the Stars and Stripes. Fifty years later, in irreverent chophouse slang, the expression signified a plate of ham and beans. In 1820 such levity would probably have been unthinkable. The flag's origin was complicated; though chosen by Congress as the national flag in 1777, it was devised in the first place as a naval ensign during the Revolutionary War and not adopted by the American

The Nation Takes Shape

army until 1834. Francis Scott Key's "Star Spangled Banner" was written in 1814, under the stimulus of a British bombardment near Baltimore, but it did not become accepted as an (unofficial) national anthem until the Civil War. The composition of the flag and the idea of adding a star for each new state while restricting the quantity of stripes to thirteen (in honor of the founding states) was not finally decided upon until 1818. However, the flag was one of the emblems of nationhood that the young United States venerated.

To a lesser extent, the American eagle was also a familiar emblem. It was the American bald eagle, a different species from the heraldic birds embodied in so many European crests. The difference was not very striking at a casual glance, and Benjamin Franklin—himself among the monuments of early American patriotism—suggested half-humorously that the turkey would have been a better choice, being "a much more respectable bird, and withal a true original native of America." However, the eagle was the preferred creature. Clutching arrows in one talon and olive branches in the other, the eagle appeared on the official seal of the United States, together with the official motto "E Pluribus Unum"; on some of the coins produced by the United States mint; and in all sorts of unofficial places as a decorative device.

Slogans, flag, eagle—though all had their importance in contributing to the image of American nationhood, none bulked as large as the Constitution. In a Fourth of July oration at New Haven in 1788 Simeon Baldwin invited his audience to

turn your attention to that venerable body [the Philadelphia Convention of 1787]—examine the characters of those illustrious sages . . . see them *unfolding* the volumes of antiquity, and carefully examining the various systems of government, which different nations have experienced, and judiciously extracting the excellence of each . . .

hear the mutual concessions of private interest to the general good, while they keep steadily in view the great object . . . and then glory, Americans, in the singular unanimity of that illustrious assembly of patriots in the most finished form of government that ever blessed a nation.

In his address Baldwin, like most other eulogists of the Constitution, emphasized its recency in order to maintain that it drew upon all previous forms of government and was therefore, as the most sophisticated model, better than all others. He also, in typical fashion, managed to speak of the Constitution as though it were an ancient affair. Less than twelve months after the Constitution had been drawn up, he talked of its makers as if they were all Methuselahs, whereas Hamilton, Madison, Edmund Randolph, and several other prominent delegates were well under forty years of age. Poetically, Baldwin's description was correct. In the American time scale, logarithmic in range at the formative stages, the Declaration of 1776 and the Constitution of 1787 tended to be represented as closer to, say, the Magna Carta of 1215 than to the actual events of the decade after 1787. The documents, being of eternal significance, were in a sense out of time altogether.

Something of this holy aura also enveloped George Washington, whose memory Bancroft invoked. His leading part in the War for Independence, his presence in the chair at the Philadelphia Convention, his imposing demeanor, and his integrity while President combined to elevate him after his death—and even during his own lifetime, though not so unanimously—to a status not far short of deification. His birthday, February 22, came second to July 4 as a national holiday. "Boston with every other considerable town in this state," wrote one of its citizens in 1796, "has marked . . . the last birthday with uncommon demonstrations of glee. It appears that our beloved President still reigns in every breast where genius, virtue, and patriotism are implanted." (Thanksgiving, which Washington ordained in 1789, was maintained as a special day by John Adams and James Madison also, but on widely varying dates; not until the Civil War did President Lincoln firmly institute the custom of an annual national Thanksgiving.) His Farewell Address of 1796, which is still read aloud in Congress every year on February 22, at once became a part of the sacred literature of American nationalism. It embodied the commandments enjoined on those who would keep the faith. Without embarrassment or thought of blasphemy, one or two writers even hinted that Washington had certain of the attributes of Jesus Christ: thus, the mother of each was named Mary, and Washington had led a singularly blameless life.

As for Bancroft's salute to "the literary prospects of America," part of what he had in mind is forcibly expressed in the words of Noah Webster. Webster, a Connecticut scholar, declared in his *Dissertations on the English Language* (1789): "A *national language* is a band of *national union*. Every engine should be employed to render the people of this country national; to call their attachments home to their own country; and to inspire them with the pride of national character. . . . Let us then seize the present moment, and establish a national language, as well as a national government." Webster felt that "Great Britain, whose children we are, and whose language we speak, should no longer be *our* standard." He did not contend that the United States should invent some entirely new tongue for herself, but rather that she should, while introducing local expressions, go back to the pure English which the mother country had corrupted. "I do not innovate but *reject innovation*," he told a correspondent in 1809. "When I write *fether, lether,* and *mold,* I do nothing more than reduce the words to their original orthography, no other being used in our earliest English books." It is a characteristic assertion in the story of American nationalism; the new land claims to be the rightful heir to an immemorial heritage; not revolution but conservation is its aim. Being mainly a lexicographer, Webster was less concerned than some authors with the wider problem of what Americans were to write about. Ardently patriotic men of letters such as Philip Freneau insisted that the national character and destiny would not be complete until there was an independent American literature. They did not necessarily mean literature devoted to the United States, but rather authorship *by* Americans, whether the field be poetry, history, philosophy, or scientific investigation.

There was similar intense concern in some circles for the development of painting, sculpture, and architecture. As with literature, the discussion involved a double argument: first, that America should have a culture respectable enough to set beside that of other nations and, second, that her culture should be unmistakably *American*—in idiom, theme, and so on. It seemed fitting that in the new "Federal City" (Washington, D.C.) an attempt was made in the Capitol building at sculptural innovation. Some of the columns in the Supreme Court wing, though based on the Corinthian principle, illustrated the leaf and blossom of the American tobacco plant, while other columns in the Senate wing rotunda were fluted like American cornstalks, with corncob capitals.

Bancroft's toast list of national symbols could be added to. There was, for instance, the cartoon symbol of "Brother

Jonathan," who seems to have originated as a contemptuous British nickname for Americans as early as 1776. The character of that name in Royall Tyler's *The Contrast* (1787)—which deserves to be regarded as the first play written by an American and staged successfully in the United States—is still a rather crudely comical person, in fact, a servant. But he is at heart honest and shrewd, like his master "Colonel Manly," and the "contrast" of the title is between them and an absurdly Anglophile master and manservant. Accepting the British taunt, the patriotic American shaped it to his own satisfaction, so that Brother Jonathan—lean, gawky, laconic, unpretentious—emerged as the caricaturist's counterpart to the fat, ruddy, blustering, conceited figure of the British "John Bull." He was a useful conception for others than writers and artists. Oddly for a nationalistic people, the Americans had no precise, convenient name for their country. "The United States" was cumbersome and sounded temporary; "America" was not a country but a continent. The obvious choice was "Columbia," which Freneau recommended and to which Joseph Hopkinson addressed his patriotic song "Hail Columbia" in 1798. But though "Columbia" sufficed eventually for the name of the federal district, of a river, of a college (in place of the old designation of "King's College"), and of another sovereign state (Colombia) on the American continent, it never lost its faintly literary taint for inhabitants of what remained, awkwardly yet permanently, the United States.

So designations like "Brother Jonathan" formed convenient synonyms as well as symbols. "Uncle Sam" was an acceptable addition. Its sense was not quite the same. Brother Jonathan represented either the whole United States or the typical individual American. Uncle Sam represented only the government of the United States. Though there are other suggested derivations, it seems to have been an extension of the initials U.S. The earliest known reference comes in a Troy, New York, newspaper in 1813: "This cant name for our government has got almost as common as 'John Bull.' The letters U.S. on the government waggons, &c are supposed to have given rise to it."

"Uncle Sam" was born in the War of 1812. The conflict made various contributions to the folklore of American nationalism. It provided some vivid fresh slogans. Young Oliver Hazard Perry, the American naval commander who defeated the British on Lake Erie in 1813, announced his victory in the famous message, "We have met the enemy and they are ours." His flagship *Lawrence* was named after an American captain who in another engagement of the war uttered as his dying words, "Don't give up the ship." These words were inscribed on Commodore Perry's flag.

Perry's and Lawrence's mottoes, like John Paul Jones's, redounded to the credit of the American navy, not the army. The regular army had its academy at West Point, whose name awoke echoes of the Revolutionary War, and there was no naval academy until the 1840's (when Bancroft, then Navy Secretary, conjured it into being). But the United States Military Academy, founded in 1802, was subject to some sharp criticism as an outpost of "aristocracy" and was not able to make an effective reply to its critics until the Mexican War. Up to 1837, neither it nor the regular army had as high a place as the navy in patriotic legend.

A special place was, however, accorded to the spectacular victory of Andrew Jackson over the British at New Orleans in 1815. Even more conclusively than Bunker Hill or Cowpens, the contest at New Orleans was held to prove that the American militiaman, the civilian warrior, was invincible. Moreover, the "Kentucky riflemen" of New Orleans were *western* heroes, a new national type whose spontaneous, rough-and-ready virtues were thought to be epitomized in their leader Jackson. He in his own right became a prime American hero—second only to Washington in éclat—who according to Bancroft "by intuitive conception . . . shared and possessed all the creative ideas of his country and his time."

The battle itself was a source of enormous pride to Americans. It set the seal on a war which, said Albert Gallatin, "has renewed . . . the national feelings and character which the Revolution had given. . . . The people have now more general objects of attachment. . . . They are more Americans; they feel and act more as a nation." The September, 1815, issue of *Niles' Register,* the first to be "printed on beautiful new type of *American* manufacture," also felt that "the people begin to assume, more and more, a NATIONAL CHARACTER; and to look at home for the only means, under divine goodness, of preserving their religion and liberty."

Some outward evidences of the American national consciousness have been indicated. To a dedicated patriot like Bancroft the United States held deeper significance. Richard Hofstadter remarks that "it has been our fate as a nation, not to have ideologies but to be one." For Bancroft, as for many of his countrymen, the American ideology had to do not only with words such as "liberty, union and democracy," but also with "providence, asylum, posterity, nature." They discerned unmistakable signs—of which one was the complete triumph at New Orleans, with shattering losses for the British and at negligible cost to Jackson's men—that the United States was under the special care of God. She had a special mission to perform, that of setting an object lesson to the rest of the world in tolerance, order, equality, and prosperity. She must therefore provide an "asylum for the oppressed"; the phrase recurs often in American speeches of the period, though not necessarily as an invitation to unlimited numbers of immigrants. The story was still being told; so its climax was invariably left to the imagination, to be disclosed fifty, a hundred, two hundred years hence, to a grateful posterity. This appeal to the future applied alike to the development of culture, commerce, population, in unlimited vistas of conjectural extrapolation.

By way of national sentiment, then, it could be said that Americans had a simultaneous attachment to yesterday and to tomorrow, the one invested with all the glamor of antiquity though its events belonged to recent history, the other with all the mysterious promise of futurity though Americans expected, so to speak, to live to see the future. However, if challenged to produce some present sign of American greatness, they could always (and did frequently) expatiate on nature in the United States. Nature meant many things—the sheer bigness of the country, the novelty of its fauna and flora, the abundance of life, the sense of room to spare, the conviction that the outdoors would be the domain of American art and letters, the definition of American character in terms of what was large, generous, informal, self-taught, non-European.

The vision was in some aspects raw and xenophobic: witness the naval officer Stephen Decatur's toast of 1816, "Our country! In her intercourse with foreign nations may she be always right; but our country, right or wrong." Thomas Low Nichols wrote of his schooling in New Hampshire in the 1820's:

> The education we got was solid enough in some respects, and superficial in others. In arithmetic, geometry, surveying, mechanics, and such solid and practical matters, we were earnest students; but our geography was chiefly American, and the United States was larger than all the universe beside. In the same way our history was American history, brief but glorious. . . . We were taught every day and in every way that ours was the freest, the happiest, and soon to be the greatest and most powerful country in the world. This is the religious faith of every American. He learns it in his infancy, and he can never forget it. For all other countries he entertains sentiments varying from pity to hatred; they are the downtrodden despotisms of the old world.

One wonders whether Nichols was exposed in the classroom to a bizarre *Historical Reader* of the War of 1812 written by Gilbert J. Hunt (1817). Hunt, whose book was designed for use in schools and went into several editions, couched it in biblical style, even breaking the chapters up into numbered verses. Thus, the President figures as "James, whose sir-name was MADISON," and Congress as "the GREAT SANHEDRIM"; Satan abets the wicked British; and, according to this latter-day American version of the holy scriptures, Jackson at New Orleans (chapter liv, verse 13)

> . . . spake, and said unto his captains of fifties, and his captains of hundreds, Fear not; we defend our lives and our liberty, and in that thing the Lord will not forsake us:
> 14. Therefore, let every man be upon his watch. . . .
> 15. And ye cunning back-woodsmen, who have known only to hunt the squirrel, the wolf, and the deer, now pour forth your strength upon the mighty lion, that we may not be overcome.
> 16. And as the black dust cast upon a burning coal instantly mounteth into a flame, so was the spirit of the husbandmen of the backwoods of Columbia.

Nationalism and Sectionalism

No doubt it was essential to reject Europe in order to form a national character; yet the rejection was accomplished by setting up a distorted image of Europe. Out of rawness, too, American patriotism was sometimes given a narrow, compulsory definition. What did not conform was denounced as un-American and therefore as verging on treason. Washington, himself, while President, came near to asserting that the political opponents of Federalism were traitorous. A generation later, efforts at the promotion of trade unions were castigated as subversive, "foreign" activities.

American nationalism was a self-conscious creation. Other nations had grown slowly; the United States had swiftly and deliberately to invent her own symbols of nationhood. The necessity was clearly understood. Note, for instance, the charge to a jury by Judge Addison of Pennsylvania, during Washington's first administration: "The laws and Constitution of our government ought to be regarded with reverence. Man must have an idol. And our political idol ought to be our Constitution and laws. They, like the ark of the covenant among the Jews, ought to be sacred from all profane touch." Robert Liston said of the nationwide memorial ceremonies held on February 22, 1800, only two months after Washington's death:

> The leading men in the United States appear to be of the opinion that these ceremonies . . . elevate the spirit of the people, and contribute to the formation of a *national* character, which they consider as much wanting in this country. And assuredly, if self-opinion is . . . an essential ingredient in that *character* which promotes the prosperity and dignity of a nation, the Americans will be gainers by the periodical recital of the feats of their Revolutionary war, and the repetition of the praises of Washington.

American nationalism was more than merely self-conscious: it was a counterstatement, a plea, a continuing debate with hostile forces. Some factors in the situation strengthened the Union; others threatened to throw it apart by centrifugal action, or at least to prevent it from becoming a fully independent nation.

To deal with the last of these groups of factors first, America's cultural nationalism suffered painful setbacks. The confidently awaited American authors and artists did not arrive on the scene as promptly as had been foretold, and when they did arrive they complained of a cool reception from their countrymen. In order to gain a hearing in the United States, they had to win a previous reputation in Europe. As poets and novelists, most of them struggled in vain to compete with Walter Scott, Byron, and a multitude of other gifted and famous Europeans. Washington Irving seemed to achieve international renown only at a price—that of becoming half-European. Fenimore Cooper, while he sturdily defended America in Europe, lived there for a prolonged interval and on returning home behaved—so his enemies thought—like one corrupted by European notions of aristocracy. These men wrote in an "English" idiom; there was hardly a sign, except in comic writing of a subliterary sort, of an "American" language. Webster's *Dictionary* and *Spelling-Book* were widely used, but his American contemporaries hesitated to adopt either the local American terms he recommended or the traditional spellings he had rediscovered. Culturally, they were alarmed by his radical *and* his conservative boldness. Some believed that America was bound to reflect her recent cultural inheritance and to reveal her cultural immaturity.

Whatever their attitudes, they were vulnerable to British jibes in the quarterly reviews and elsewhere. Seen unsympathetically, American cultural pretensions were absurd; to appreciate the full overtones of the American predicament called for more detachment than either side could usually muster. One of the ironies, for example, was that the corncob capital, symbol of native genius, was carved by an Italian craftsman imported by Jefferson to work on the embellishments to the new Capitol. For that matter, most of the early patriotic statuary, from Houdon's figure of George Washington to the productions of Causici or Canova, was commissioned from foreigners. Another irony was that despite outbursts of belligerent nationalism, the United States was surprisingly reluctant to commemorate her heroes or heroic episodes. In part her caution arose from a feeling that it was dangerous to the cause of republicanism to pay too much tribute to individuals, in part from low aesthetic standards among congressmen, and in part from the erratic ways of American government. Though the Continental Congress voted an equestrian statue to George Washington some years before he became President, it was not finished until fifty years after he was dead; and the Washington Monument, projected in 1800, took even longer to complete. Jefferson did not get his memorial in Washington, D.C.—admittedly a lavish one when it came—until he had been in the grave a full century. John Browere, an American who took life masks in plaster of Jefferson and others in order to compile a national portrait gallery, exhausted his savings in the task and could not persuade President Madison to provide money for casting the likenesses in bronze. Browere's collection was not rescued from oblivion until the very end of the nineteenth century, when it was found tucked away in a New York farmhouse.

But such slights were trivial in comparison with the immediate dangers to the Union. During the administrations of

Washington, Adams, Jefferson, and Madison there were successive moves to dismember some portion or other of the Union, and the menace returned, after a crisis weathered by Monroe, to darken the presidency of Andrew Jackson.

The nature of the peril changed with time. At the outset of the period the most likely threat was posed by what we might call separatism, while by Jackson's time the major risk was beginning to come from sectionalism. There was also, of course, the possibility that the early Union might simply disintegrate, out of failure to cohere. National loyalty was a novel sentiment. Though they might admire the Constitution, many were suspicious of the federal government and would make its authority minimal. Loyalty to the individual states, at least for the original thirteen, was a habit of far longer standing; and during the first half-century under the Constitution the individual states by no means lost their nerve—as their vigorous economic activities made plain.

However, the early challenge to the Union—or for that matter the later one—did not come from any single state, although the state-rights controversy was couched in terms that might imply as much. It came rather from the weakly attached, peripheral areas. Rhode Island, which refused initially to ratify the Constitution, might have indulged in separatist maneuvers if it had lain on the outer edge of the United States. Its geographical situation, hedged in by Massachusetts and Connecticut, made any move of that kind impossible.

No such practical inhibition controlled other areas, or the adventurers who saw chances for themselves. One of the alarming features of the first generation of independence was that some of the very men whose courage and confidence fitted them to be national heroes were also those most tempted to turn their backs on the Union. Benedict Arnold's was the first defection; it was a blow to Washington and the whole American cause when Arnold attempted to betray West Point to the British in 1780. Ethan Allen, another of the cocksure patriots, became involved before his death in 1789 in dubious negotiations with British Canada over the fate of his native province of Vermont. George Rogers Clark, a third hero of the Revolutionary War, fell into disgrace while holding the post of Indian commissioner, on the ground that he had entered a western separatist conspiracy. It seems that in his case the accusation was unjust, but Americans of his day were ready to believe it.

The whole western frontier—everything that lay beyond the Appalachians—was held to the United States by the loosest ties. It could easily fall to Britain, to Spain (or France), or it could break away from the United States and maintain itself as one or more independent countries. This possibility worried George Washington in particular. With a long experience of western issues, he saw in the maintenance of a powerful union the best hope of avoiding western separatism.

A sequence of adventurers held opposite views. One of the busiest and most disreputable was James Wilkinson of Kentucky, later a general in the American army. A couple of years before Washington's inauguration, Wilkinson, who had secured a trade monopoly to sell Kentucky produce in (Spanish) New Orleans, became implicated in a scheme to prevent Kentucky, not yet a state, from joining the Union. In his plan, Kentucky would stand aloof and come to terms with her Spanish neighbors. The plan—sometimes alluded to as the "Spanish Conspiracy"—evaporated. Kentucky became a state in 1792. But Wilkinson was put secretly on the Spanish pension list at $2,000 a year; he seems to have been responsible for Clark's disgrace; and he remained an equivocal figure until he and Aaron Burr were accused in 1805–6 of having plotted to establish a southwestern empire. Burr, incidentally, claimed long afterward that he "never got within ten thousand leagues of a wish to break up the United States by a separatist or a secession movement, although I did hope to establish an empire in Mexico and become its emperor." In the meantime the French republican minister Genêt had concocted some abortive western projects in 1793; and a few years later Senator William Blount of Tennessee, an influential speculator, evolved an elaborate expedition—on paper—in which a combined force of American frontiersmen and British troops from Canada were to pick up some of the southern Indians en route and then overrun Spanish Florida and Louisiana. The plot, if it can be called that, was revealed and Blount was expelled from the Senate. But he was so popular in his own state that it proved impossible to arrest him, let alone bring him to trial.

None of these brain children came to birth. The last hopes of carving out independent frontier realms seemed to die with the American acquisition of Louisiana and Florida. However, something of the earlier spirit, half vision, half confidence-trick, survived in the American settlement of Texas during the 1820's (and in the later filibustering enterprises of the 1850's). The difference was that by then separatism was yielding to sectionalism. In 1804, a little after the Louisiana Purchase, Jefferson could still coolly remark that "whether we remain in one confederacy, or form into Atlantic and Mississippi confederacies, I believe not very important to the happiness of either part. Those of the Western confederacy will be as much our children and descendants as those of the Eastern, and I feel myself as much identified with that country in future as with this." It is hard to interpret the observation properly. To some extent Jefferson spoke for himself, in the detached role of student of human affairs. He was, too, the spokesman of a western viewpoint, a little guilty as to the constitutional propriety of having bought Louisiana and perhaps (even though he maintained that the theory did not apply to a representative, federal government like the United States) worried by Montesquieu's warning that large republics are doomed to disunion: better a cheerful acquiescence in the prospect than a futile contest to avert it.

At any rate, the quotation is untypical. The Union did become more closely knit. The ingredients of nationalism took effect. The new states in the West, created from federal territory, were quick to declare their fealty to the Union. Improved communications, especially with the advent of the railroad, seemed to make nonsense of theories like Montesquieu's. At least, this was the contention of a persuasive nationalist like John C. Calhoun of South Carolina in 1817: "The more enlarged the sphere of commercial circulation—the more extended that of social intercourse—the more strongly are we bound together—the more inseparable are our destinies. . . . Let us, then, bind the republic together with a perfect system of roads and canals. Let us conquer space."

By the time Calhoun delivered this speech in the House of Representatives, there was no serious risk left of a division between West and East. The West was becoming a self-conscious section, but only in relation to the Atlantic states, which were competing for its commercial affections. The problems of the West were now defined as extensions of those of the East and those soon to be argued between North and South. Americans were ceasing to speak without qualification of the "East" or of the "Atlantic states." The meaningful sections were West, North, and South, and the last two were at variance.

Their rivalry was not an unfamiliar feature. In colonial days, when it was customary to conceive of a tripartite division—New England, the Middle Colonies, the South—this grouping was more than simply geographical. While each colony tended to be prejudiced against all the others, there were marked antipathies between New England and the South. The Yankee, "Solomon Swap," was seen as a dry, joyless, falsely pious, cheating tradesman (an opinion partially held by inhabitants of the Middle Colonies also). The southerner was envisaged as an immoral, dueling, unlettered slaveholder. Under the new Constitution, as rivalry developed between the followers of Hamilton and those of Jefferson and Madison, the middle states—New York, New Jersey, Pennsylvania—gradually became aligned with those of New England, as areas with a diversified and commercialized economy. The South, increasingly engrossed in its cotton staple and in the institution of slavery on which cotton was thought to depend, took on more and more the semblance of a distinct region.

On issue after issue Congress split along roughly sectional lines. In 1792 there was an argument over the reapportionment of seats in the House of Representatives. Two different methods were proposed by northern and southern members, each bloc naturally seeking its own advantage in the dispute. Jefferson favored the southern bill. Consulted by President Washington, he recommended a veto of the northern bill, which Washington eventually decided upon. But, says Jefferson, the President "observed that the vote for & against the bill was perfectly geographical, a northern [against] a southern vote, & he feared he should be thought to be taking side with a southern party. I admitted this motive of delicacy, but [urged] that it should not induce him to do wrong. . . . He here expressed his fear that there would be ere long, a separation of the union; that the public mind seemed dissatisfied & tending to this."

To this dread, after observing American political animosities during four further painful years in office, Washington reverted in his Farewell Address. Surely, he insisted, "the name of American, which belongs to you in your national capacity, must always exalt the just pride of patriotism more than any appellation derived from local discriminations. With slight shades of difference, you have the same religion, manners, habits, and political principles." Each of the main geographical regions benefited from the activities of the others. It was lamentable that "any ground should have been furnished for characterizing parties by *geographical* discriminations—*Northern* and *Southern*, *Atlantic* and *Western*—whence designing men may endeavor to excite a belief that there is a real difference of local interests and views."

Forty years later, in a second farewell address to the people of the United States, Andrew Jackson reiterated the anxieties voiced in Washington's "imperishable document." "Atlantic" and "Western" had disappeared as antagonistic forces; nevertheless,

We behold systematic efforts publicly made to sow the seeds of discord between different parts of the United States and to place party divisions directly upon geographical distinctions; to excite the *south* against the *north* and the *north* against the *south* . . . and the possible dissolution of the Union has at length become . . . a familiar subject of discussion.

Jackson was alluding to a particular and recent crisis. Yet the possible dissolution of the Union had been a constant topic of discussion, if usually by way of warning, ever since Washington—the theme touched on in almost every Independence Day oration and at some stage or other in practically every debate in Congress. For a number of years before the War of 1812 there had been mounting dissatisfaction in New England at Jeffersonian policies that the "Essex Junto" saw as aimed directly against the interests of the region. During the conflict itself, New England displayed both passive and active resentment at "Mr. Madison's war." The idea of a northern confederacy had been mooted as early as 1804. New Yorkers showed little disposition to join it, though there too the war of 1812 was unpopular: "Uncle Sam's" wagons did not exhilarate bystanders as they rumbled toward Canada. However, the leading malcontents in New England summoned a convention that met at Hartford, Connecticut, at the end of 1814, to consider revisions of the Constitution. The convention did not propose secession from the Union. But it expressed an extreme state-rights position, similar to that upheld in 1798 by the Republican legislatures of Kentucky and Virginia in protest at the Alien and Sedition Acts passed under John Adams' Federalist administration. Now Federalist New England used the Republican arguments against a Republican administration.

The news of the Treaty of Ghent, ending the war, and of Jackson's feat at New Orleans, reached New England soon after the close of the Hartford deliberations and robbed them of their impact. Peace had been secured and honor was intact. In face of such news, the indignation of the Hartford delegates sounded querulous. The mood of sectional defiance did not take long to disappear in the North.

Nationalism and Sectionalism

It reappeared in the South. Most of the Atlantic states harbored grievances, as they continued to yield population and influence to the West. On this score Massachusetts had as much cause for complaint as Virginia or South Carolina. New England had other grudges against the South. After the War of 1812, the "Virginia dynasty" showed no signs of losing authority in the federal government. Politics were swayed by sectional issues but not dominated by sectionalism. According to the distinguished historian Charles S. Sydnor, the South in 1819 was "unawakened"—far less conscious of itself as a section than was New England.

The first major sectional crisis, that of 1819–21, awakened the South and consoled the North. Hitherto, new states had joined the Union in North-South pairs—Vermont and Kentucky, Indiana and Mississippi—but without any very serious sectional intent. The habit became a matter of urgent principle over the question of statehood for Missouri, the first state to be carved from the Louisiana Purchase. Eventually Missouri joined the Union as a slave state at the same time that Maine entered as a free state. Henceforward the South would accept new free states only if they were paired off with slave states, thus perpetuating what was an exact equality in numbers.

The geographical south did not become the sectional South overnight. But each year, as New England and the North forged farther ahead in numbers and wealth, the sectional equation grew in importance. When Monroe left the presidency, the days of the Virginia dynasty were over. The northern seaboard states forgot their grievances; the southern ones remembered theirs. Yet political parity, at least in the Senate if not in the House of Representatives, could be maintained so long as admissions to the Union were properly balanced.

The Nation Takes Shape

The South could also hope to win the sympathies and the trade of the West. Or rather, such a hope was plausible until the canal and the railroad began to pull commerce eastward instead of downriver to New Orleans. As late as 1830, Senator Benton of Missouri was proclaiming that his state looked toward the South, not to the cities of the Atlantic. After that date not many western spokesmen defined their allegiance thus. The Old South, committed to slavery, a prey to painful disappointments, fought every real or imagined encroachment upon its dwindling empire.

The tariff became for southern leaders a crucial issue. Here, they were convinced, the commercial North, not content with drawing off the profits from southern agriculture by less obvious devices, sought to impose a tax upon farmer and planter solely to protect the northern manufacturer. When the Tariff of 1828—the "Tariff of Abominations"—passed Congress, South Carolina resisted. John C. Calhoun, its distinguished son, had altered his opinions; he was now sure that the North had captured the federal government and that sectionalism was the only answer.

Calhoun took the logic of sectionalism further than the Essex Junto. The protests that he wrote for his state were seconded by Georgia, Mississippi, and Virginia. The question hung fire for some time. Then in 1832 there was furious controversy between the federal government and the forces of union in South Carolina on the one hand and the Calhoun doctrine of "nullification" on the other. A state convention in South Carolina nullified recent tariff acts and declared its defiance of Jackson's administration. Only after months of threats and counterthreats did the contestants reach a tacit compromise, by which the federal government undertook to reduce the tariff and the South Carolina legislature suspended its nullification ordinance.

This was the background to Andrew Jackson's farewell address. A few months before he spoke, a book was published, with the fictitious date 1856 upon the title page, called *The Partisan Leader*. The pseudonymous work of N. B. Tucker, a professor at William and Mary College in Virginia, it was a fantasy foretelling the secession of South Carolina. In the same year the Texans gained their independence from Mexico. But "Remember the Alamo!" did not become a national slogan; the nation was too deeply divided to welcome the prospect of gaining Texas as a new, slaveholding member of the Union. "To me," declared W. E. Channing of Massachusetts in 1837, "it seems not only the right but the duty of the free states, in case of the annexation of Texas, to say to the slave-holding states, 'We regard this act as the dissolution of the Union.'"

How can all this be reconciled with enthusiastic nationalism? Certainly there was a major contradiction within American society, this "piebald polity," in Thomas Moore's phrase, "of slaving blacks and democratic whites." The situation is accurately expressed by Tocqueville's image of nationalism and sectionalism as two separate currents "flowing in contrary directions in the same channel." Both were strong currents. Both were, in a way, artificial currents. If it was comforting to reflect that sectionalism might prove merely a temporary phase, it was disturbing to realize that the same might be said of American nationalism. Most Americans contrived to believe in both *ism*'s, simultaneously or in rapid succession, as the situation dictated.

The Union had gained enormously in strength and coherence during the half-century. Washington referred to it as an "experiment." When Jackson claimed that the experiment had succeeded, he was correct by every index of material well-being. The affection for the Union shown by the new states and the nationwide enthusiasm aroused by Lafayette's visit in 1825 were heartening signs of solidarity. We should not exaggerate the extent of sectional feeling—or of its somewhat incompatible companion, desire for state sovereignty—before 1837. The states that lifted their voices in support of South Carolina did so only in a ragged, wavering, and quickly silenced chorus. Even Calhoun's own South Carolina was far from unanimous in its defiance of the federal government. The many Americans who, on one occasion or another, raised the specter of secession were fully aware of the awfulness of the threat. They could be compared to men in the Middle Ages who achieved a similar effect by invoking the devil.

More compelling than all the symbols of Americanism, however, were the physical evidences of the nation's prosperity. It was an unequal prosperity; the West and South were less well provided than the North with schools, colleges, hospitals, jails, and other signs of high civilization. But they too were growing, active regions. The United States, clearly, was a going concern, whose inhabitants' noisy verbal warfare with one another testified to an essential vigor. Nor should we overlook the relative unconcern of many Americans. They were a busy people, engrossed in local and day-to-day problems. Often they remained indifferent to what was being fought over by their legislators. They could be aroused to fury, but their emotions died away rapidly.

It was also true, as Jackson admitted, that the foundations of union "must be laid in the affections of the people." American nationalism had still to be expressed as an imperative; yet he knew that in the last analysis unity could not be enforced. Washington failed to appreciate this fully, so concerned was he to deny that any significant diversities ought to exist in the United States. By Jackson's day Americans were accustomed to the inescapable reality. The country *was* divided; behind the formal niceties of constitutional theory were shifting coalitions of interests. The task of American politics was to reach acceptable compromises. The prayer of American patriots was that the American "national character"—in the ambiguous terminology they employed—would also be a nationalist character. In any case, the search for American identity—national, sectional, individual—would no doubt be protracted. Mercifully, perhaps, the average American remained unaware that he was living in a quandary. There was much to be said for simply ignoring problems in the hope that they would eventually go away. Of no other country could it be so plausibly maintained that matter-of-factness was on occasion more valuable than intellectual discourse.

VII

Conservatism and Democracy

How has the growth of American democracy within this period usually been explained? We might concoct a composite interpretation, according to prevalent twentieth-century textbook doctrine, as follows: The Revolution was a double struggle, fought within each colony as well as by the colonies against the mother country. It was inspired by the "democratic" faith voiced in the Declaration of Independence. But misgivings assailed the more "conservative" elements in America, who had no wish to yield power to mobs and landless men. The self-styled "wise and the good" therefore drafted a cautious new Constitution; and under the Federalist administrations of Washington and John Adams, by means of a strong, centralized, money-minded government, by restricted franchises and other artificial restraints, they upheld their notion of an incompletely democratic America. They were encouraged in this attitude by their colonial heritage, for the class distinctions of Britain had in less extreme form taken root across the Atlantic. They were still more encouraged to stand fast by the events of the 1790's in France, where the effects of thoroughgoing revolution were horribly plain for all to see.

However (to continue with this orthodox composite explanation), the Federalists were stiff and unyielding. They misjudged the temper of America in 1798, when the Alien and Sedition Acts were passed, and they steadily lost ground in the next few years. They hung on longest in New England, particularly in the "Essex Junto" of Massachusetts, which carried disgruntled conservatism almost to the point of treason. Crotchety, snobbish, anachronistic survivals from another era, they were driven from political power first in the federal government and then in state after state.

Their views triumphed temporarily, in diluted or oblique guises. Though the Federalists dwindled as a national party in the "revolution" of 1800, their economic, political, and social doctrines were enshrined in the Supreme Court, and to some extent in the Republican administrations of Jefferson and his successors. Jefferson spoke more truly than he realized when, in an effort at tact, he proclaimed in his first inaugural address (1801) that "we are all Republicans, we are all Federalists." The conservatism of circumstance, the weight of special interests, combined to weaken the democratic creed. When the Bank of the United States was chartered in 1791, Jefferson and Madison protested vehemently at the unwarranted innovation and its dangerous implications for a would-be egalitarian society. Twenty years later, when the Bank's charter expired, both men unsuccessfully pleaded for its renewal.

The result of the War of 1812 was to fasten upon the Republicans additional "Federalist" encumbrances. It raised the national debt and impelled the federal government to exert energies better reserved to the individual states. Another, second Bank of the United States had to be created in 1816. But in the aftermath, freed from a quarter-century of anxiety, the nation returned to the interrupted theme of perfect democracy.

The transition took time. The issues were complex, the lines of division indistinct. Yet (so we have been told), during the "era of good feeling" that characterized Madison's later years and the two administrations of James Monroe (i.e., from 1815 to 1825), the lines were redrawn. As new western states came into the Union, their constitutions showed a move toward full-scale democracy, typified in the provision for unrestricted male suffrage and for popularly elected state officials. Some older states revealed the same tendency. But the full impulse was still checked. It appeared prematurely in the election of 1824, with the emergence on the national scene of Andrew Jackson, "Old Hickory" from Tennessee. Narrowly defeated—in fact not defeated in popular esteem but a victim of political machinations in Congress—he bided his time from 1825 to the election of 1828, while John Quincy Adams from the White House gazed aghast at the rising tide of Jacksonian Democracy. Political allegiances were now recast, until Jackson had a nationwide movement behind him. Political practices were reformed. The private bargaining of the caucus system began to give way to the more open and popular "convention," at which the will of the people was harder to muffle.

In 1828 Jackson was victorious. Inaugurated the next March, he brought in a reign of the people, symbolized by John Quincy Adams' refusal to participate in the ceremony (his father John Adams had absented himself from Jefferson's inauguration) and by the crowd of spectators who surged into the White House, where, jostling democratically to catch a glimpse of their hero, they stood in their symbolic muddy boots upon the symbolic satin upholstery of the presidential furniture. Tough, self-made, western, unconventional, this man—we are told—personified the Declaration of Independence.

Some of the manifestations of political democracy were unfortunate. The campaign of 1824 was the most scurrilous America had known—until that of 1828. Nor was the spoils system, of rewarding faithful party men by appointing them to office through the wholesale ejection of previous incumbents, altogether praiseworthy. But these were only to be expected. In other respects the gospel of equality nobly completed the work begun fifty years before. In the *second* American revolution the "party of privilege" was overthrown. Franchises were extended. Tariffs were lowered. After 1835, under a new Chief Justice—Roger B. Taney—who was a Jackson man, the Supreme Court showed signs of countermanding the sternly contractual Federalist code of John Marshall. The "conservative" influence of the "Monster" Bank of the United States ("B.U.S." for short) was annihilated in a spectacular controversy. There were other evidences of the upsurge of Jacksonian Democracy. For example, imprisonment for debt was abolished in Massachusetts in 1834, and the news was announced on that day of national celebration, July 4.

The triumph of Jackson paradoxically led to the temporary eclipse of his Democratic party. For in 1840 the rival Whig party, which had also emerged from the welter of old-fashioned Republicanism, paid the Jacksonian movement the compliment of imitation—in fact, emulation. In a campaign aimed at the people, the People with a capital *P,* the Whigs took over the trappings of Democracy, indeed also democracy with a small *d.*

The Nation Takes Shape

This, to reiterate, is the kind of interpretation that has been usually though not universally applied to American history from Washington to Jackson. It is to be found in Carl Russell Fish, *The Rise of the Common Man, 1830–1850* (1927), a volume in the "History of American Life" series in which, the general editors claim by way of introduction, "Professor Fish shows American society in the process of remaking itself. The cultural heritage of the American people during these years was essentially an aristocratic one; even the efforts of the preceding generation for cultural independence [the generation from 1790 to 1830] had affected little in the life of the masses." Or in Frederick Jackson Turner's *Rise of the New West* (1906) we may read of "the formation of the self-conscious American democracy," which "came to its own when Andrew Jackson triumphed over the old order of things."

In recent years the picture has been subjected to critical scrutiny. One or two historians have attacked the problem at its origins. Thus, two volumes by Robert E. Brown, *Middle-Class Democracy and the Revolution in Massachusetts, 1691–1780* (1955) and *Beard and the Constitution* (1956), bear upon our period though chronologically they lie outside it. Brown's thesis is that Massachusetts, and probably the rest of the United States, were well advanced in democracy by the time of the Revolution; that, contrary to the celebrated interpretation of Charles A. Beard, the federal Constitution of 1787 was *not* the "conservative" document of a prosperous, educated minority managing to perpetuate and extend its privileges, but a sensible program, "democratically" sanctioned by state conventions; and that in short the "common man" may have "come into his own long before the era of Jacksonian Democracy."

Brown and others have reminded us of the testimony of early

Conservatism and Democracy

European travelers, as well as of better-informed observers like Franklin and Crèvecœur. American society, says Crèvecœur's hypothetical American farmer as early as 1782, is not composed as in Europe of

> great lords who possess everything, and of a herd of people who have nothing. Here are no aristocratical families, no courts, no kings, no bishops, no ecclesiastical dominion, no invisible power giving to a few a very visible one; no great manufacturers employing thousands, no great refinements of luxury. . . . We are the most perfect society now existing in the world. Here man is free as he ought to be.

Similar comments by visiting Europeans could be quoted from Revolutionary times up to the retirement of Andrew Jackson. Not all admired what they saw. Some dwelt with relief on the polite society to be found on southern plantations, or in the homes of the wealthy in New York or Boston, or in the company of such men of letters (a small group) as Joseph Dennie of Philadelphia, or among the ambitious hostesses of Washington. Some remarked acidly that, despite American statements to the contrary, there were after all signs—whether vestigial or embryonic—of class distinction in the New World. Some shuddered at the coarse intimacies of the stagecoach, the steamboat, the backwoods tavern. Some were irked by or amused at the lack of deference shown them, as when the Honorable Charles Augustus Murray, who journeyed through America during Jackson's second administration, was addressed by his host as "Charlie" on the very evening of his arrival at one place. But all testified to the existence of a social order with relatively few grades of rank and with no one (save free man and slave) fundamentally isolated from another.

The impression that "democracy" predated the presidency of Jackson appears to be sustained by a good deal of additional evidence. For instance, property-holding and taxpaying qualifications for voting were abolished by New Jersey in 1807 and by Maryland in 1810. In widening the franchise and extending its elective scope, the constitutions of new states like Indiana (1816), Illinois (1818), and Alabama (1819) were equally "democratic" in their provisions. So were the new or amended constitutions of Connecticut (1818), Massachusetts (1820), and New York (1821). In Connecticut, where the "Toleration" movement overthrew the established Congregational church and its alliance with Federalist laymen, the change was possibly of some consequence. But in Massachusetts the amendments approved a couple of years later did little more than formally sanction "democratic" voting habits that had been informally sanctioned for a generation. And in New York, for all the fire and fury of contending orators, the battle was without deep significance.

It seems reasonable to suppose, then, that we must date the origins of the Jacksonian movement earlier than has been commonly done. But what of full-fledged Jacksonian Democracy? We need to look further at its nature, both for the period 1815–28, when "Jacksonism" (as it was also called) saw the transformation of a national military hero into a successful presidential candidate, and for the next eight years, when it was a working presidential program. We need to consider whether Jackson's attitudes changed in and out of office, whether they represent any evolution from previous aspects of American "democracy," and what in any case we mean by this unusably vague yet unavoidably crucial concept of "democracy," with its almost equally unusable and unavoidable yokefellow "conservatism." For the moment we may beg that difficult question and turn instead to consider American politics before 1829 in the light of the conventional interpretation summarized at the beginning of the chapter.

Perhaps that is the wrong way to put it, for the light turns out to be too benignly clear. Recent examinations of political activity in such states as Pennsylvania, Ohio, and Tennessee have confirmed that the "era of good feeling" witnessed plenty of bad feeling. Local politicians waged their intricate guerrilla campaigns on local issues. Fierce rivalries arose, such as that between Pittsburgh and Philadelphia within Pennsylvania, or between Philadelphia and Baltimore or New York outside state boundaries. Within the various states, the upcountry or western areas tended to struggle against the older, eastern areas of settlement (in Tennessee, where the eastern areas were mountainous and therefore more thinly populated than the western, the pattern was reversed). But even here, where we seem for a moment to recognize the familiar western-eastern, democratic-conservative polarity which served as the motif for much of Frederick Jackson Turner's attractive theorizing, the conflict proves far from simple. A false simplicity was imparted by the relation of local and state to national politics. As foreign visitors noted, local men liked to base their appeals on national figures, if not national issues—on a Henry Clay, a John Quincy Adams, or an Andrew Jackson. But the patchwork of special interests was, rather, a crazy quilt of disharmonies and contradictions.

In the 1824 election, discounting personalities, there was little to choose between Clay, Adams, and Jackson. The first two stood for a somewhat greater degree of federal intervention in order to develop the Union: for "internal improvements" and for a tariff to provide adequate revenue and to protect small manufacturers or producers. But their intentions were not bas-

ically different from Jackson's. Like Clay, Jackson was a westerner; but like Clay again, he was no Davy Crockett. Actually,
a few years afterward Davy Crockett himself, having been a
Jackson man, swung against his chief and lent his vernacular,
coonskin talents to the cause of Jackson's Whig enemies. General Jackson was a conspicuous target for those who chose to
question his role as spokesman of democracy. Slaveholder,
landowner, man of property, impatient litigant when the need
arose, brusque creditor devoid of sympathy for those who
could not or would not pay their debts, he could easily if not
with entire justice be caricatured as "King Andrew"—the very
opposite of a "democrat."

As Crockett's desertion suggests, there was a bewildering
kaleidoscope of loyalties, programs, ambitions, antipathies. In
1824, and again somewhat less strikingly in 1828, there was not
much difference between the supporters of the respective candidates. The candidate's reputation and personality (or what
was known or conjectured of these) counted for much. Each
had his fervent admirers among political managers and among
the public. To some the integrity of Adams commended itself,
to others the charm of Clay, to others the bravura of Jackson.
There was, as might be expected, some sectional alignment in
favor of each—Tennessee for Jackson, New England for
Adams, and so on. But each had opponents within his own
area.

Neither enmities nor allegiances were fixed or predictable.
There was nothing to guarantee that a man would not vote,
say, the Adams ticket in his own state, yet support Clay or
Jackson for the presidency. There was not much to show
which way prominent subordinates would turn. For example,
Senator Thomas Hart Benton of Missouri, who in 1813 had

been involved in a bloody fracas with Jackson, who was related by marriage to Henry Clay, and who was associated in his state with the "St. Louis Junto" of conservative speculators, nevertheless cast in his lot with Jackson. He could have taken other directions, with as great a degree of honesty or common sense.

To choose another situation, there was little logic save in political expediency to the rise of the Antimasonic party of these years. The creation of Thurlow Weed and other astute politicians in New York, it spread swiftly into adjacent states though its only basis was dislike of the secret, fraternal order known as Freemasonry—and, by extension, of secret cabals of any sort. A good, hearty, Jacksonian prejudice, one would have thought. But Jackson himself was, it chanced, a Mason; so, since Weed was an Adams follower, the party served as an anti-Jackson force. Except again for political expediency, there was no overriding reason why Van Buren should with the rest of the "Albany Regency" of New York have plumped for Jackson. Nor why, except in part for hostility to the Regency, Thurlow Weed, the son of a poor man whose imprisonments for debt he vividly recalled, should not have been a warrior in the Jackson camp fighting for Democracy.

True, New York politics, with their Tammany, "Loco-Foco," and kindred factions, were even more involved than those of other states. Oliver Wolcott, who served as Secretary of the Treasury from 1795 to 1800, subsequently became a well-to-do New York businessman. Later, having returned to his native Connecticut, Wolcott wrote of New York:

After living a dozen years in that State, I don't pretend to comprehend their politics. It is a labyrinth of wheels within wheels, and is understood only by the managers. Why, these leaders of the opposite parties, who—in the papers and before the world—seem ready to tear each other's eyes out, will meet some rainy night in a dark entry, and agree, whichever way the election goes, they will share the spoils together.

As this quotation reminds us, New York pioneered the spoils system (though it had not been unknown to Jefferson also) and passed it on to Andrew Jackson as a vital component of popular government.

But New York was merely the prize example, not the only example, of the labyrinthine relations between state and nation, between politics and democracy. Wolcott's own career is instructive. In the cabinets of Washington and John Adams he was a staunch Federalist, a Hamiltonian. Yet in 1817 he was nominated and elected to the governorship of Connecticut as a champion of reform. The resulting debate, in Samuel G. Goodrich's recollection, was "one of the most violent that was ever witnessed in Connecticut. It was curious as well as violent—for we saw fighting side by side, shoulder to shoulder, democracy, Methodism, Episcopacy, Pedobaptism, radicalism, infidelity—all united for the overthrow of federalism and orthodoxy; and Oliver Wolcott was the leader in this onset!" Even more peculiar, the passions aroused in the struggle died down in a short space of time.

Many another seeming oddity could be mentioned. No one would have expected a son of Alexander Hamilton to become an ardent Tammany Democrat and close associate of Andrew Jackson—Jackson, the man who felt that Aaron Burr had been wronged. Yet this was the behavior of James A. Hamilton, who in diametric opposition to his Federalist father's views assisted Jackson in pulling down the Bank of the United States. Nor do we readily recall that Nicholas Biddle of that same bank, execrated by the Jacksonians as a scheming aristocrat, had in Madison's time been accounted a good Republican, or—a sharper irony—that in 1828, admittedly to the surprise of his acquaintances, he preferred Jackson to Adams.

There are still earlier curiosities. John Marshall, while a Federalist in 1793, confessed that his political opinions of that date were tinctured with "wild and enthusiastic democracy." Wolcott's cabinet colleague Timothy Pickering had been a vigorous Republican until about 1795, when he abruptly changed sides, to the disgust of his friends, and became a Federalist. Fluctuations mark the public career of another contemporary New Englander, Elbridge Gerry of Massachusetts, whom a colleague once described as "the veriest quiddle in nature." An Antifederalist before 1789, he was then for some years a loyal Adams Federalist, and then later a Republican. Fisher Ames of the same state remained a firm and outstandingly eloquent Federalist until his death in 1808; yet his brother Nathaniel was so implacable a Republican that he even refused to attend Fisher's funeral, alleging that the affair was being staged as a Federalist pageant.

These hints at the complexity of American political beliefs should be enough to demonstrate that there was never a straightforward cleavage between Hamiltonianism and Jeffersonianism, or any other pair of isms current in the period. They suggest that Jacksonian Democracy ought to be viewed as a political phenomenon rather than as a crusade of the poor and needy against the rich and greedy.

Interpreted thus, the era would seem to be lacking in genuine ideological clashes. That supposition might explain the role of personality in political preference, personality divorced from or independent of political hue—the voter discerning in the personality of the candidate both his own likeness and the intimation of some quality more grandly American. It might explain the curious explorations by political leaders in search of principles on which to stand: principles, that is, not as beliefs so much as tactical advantages, like the seizure of high ground by one army engaged in combat with another. Hence the wistful sigh in 1821 of a senator friendly to William H. Crawford of Georgia, anxious to push him for the presidency in 1824: "Could we only hit upon a few great principles and unite their support with that of Crawford, we should succeed beyond doubt." Here is the personality—or rather the personality's friend—in search of the principle with which to link him. Hence, too, the efforts of Van Buren in the 1820's to build up the old bastion of state rights into a fortress for Jacksonians, even though few of their voting records justified him, strictly speaking. Hence the glee of Benton in 1831 at reconnoitering a really admirable means of attack against the "Monster Bank" in defense of what he called the "*demos krateo* principle": "The B.U.S. is the turning point. That political engine of the federal monarchical party, will draw the lines between parties again."

As a candidate, Jackson was not very explicit. In office he spoke up more clearly on certain matters. But in both cases it is noteworthy that he and his followers emphasized conservation quite as much as innovation. The philosopher George Santayana once argued, in another context, that "America is not simply . . . a young country with an old mentality: it is a country with two mentalities, one a survival of the beliefs and standards of the fathers, the other an expression of the instincts, practice, and discoveries of the younger generations." Andrew

Jackson would seem a case in point. He would seem, if we may continue to employ words that are so slippery to handle, "conservative" in several respects if "democratic" in others. Once elected, he and such supporters in Congress as Benton, or James K. Polk of Tennessee, together with publicists like George Bancroft, did make a bold plea for popular government, for a land in which all free men were to be still more free. Yet the America he envisaged was a land of yeomen. The Americans he admired, whose praises he sang, were not enterprising merchants and manufacturers, nor yet pioneers hacking out the wilderness in primitive isolation, but peaceful, settled, freeholding farmers: men of middling fortune, decent, Arcadian: men who would stay put, having once got where they must go, and mix their labor with the land.

The virtuous husbandman was a Jeffersonian ideal. It was not by any means a fantastic dream in Jefferson's day, and it still had real and reasonable elements in the era of Jackson. Not only was there ample precedent for belief in the stability of communities composed of such citizens; freeholding farmers actually did comprise a large proportion of the American population up to 1837.

But among the things that American democracy implied was a constantly changing and expanding economy. This was the dynamic of democracy—a perpetual mild discontent, an itch to try the cards at the next table, the view from the next ridge. In an open society men would not stay still, literally or metaphorically. As early as 1794 Moreau de St. Méry, a Frenchman living in New York, noted that people there had a "mania" for moving every year, on May 1, from one rented house to another hardly distinguishable at a casual glance. Even if American farmers lived well in closely knit communities on fertile soil, they were likely to pull up stakes and try for improved circumstances somewhere else. The process testified to the vigor and freedom of American society: no mortmain here, no shackles of entail and primogeniture, no chronic landlordism. Jackson's own career showed what could be accomplished by an American, by *any* American, who had the energy to move, to speculate, to embark on fresh enterprises.

But the craving for mobility makes a strange juxtaposition with the sober, almost archaic message of Jacksonian Democracy. After all, the proportion of farmers was diminishing yearly as cities grew and as areas became more thickly inhabited. The emotional appeal of Jacksonianism both embraced and excluded the urban working man. The same could be said of the self-made entrepreneurs of his generation (and, incidentally, the word "self-made" belongs to Jackson's time; Henry Clay appears to have introduced it in 1832, in the course of a Senate speech).

Perhaps the answer can be framed as a paraphrased aphorism. Nostalgia, we could say, is the tribute that laissez-faire democracy paid to republican conservatism, that capitalist enterprise paid to agrarian Arcadia. There is no reason to doubt that Jackson and his lieutenants were sincere when they campaigned for a new order which was in some ways the old order restored. It was an attitude that commended itself to many Americans made uneasy by the very progress they applauded. Those who supported Jackson liked to believe he had hit upon the right balance between yesterday and tomorrow. He had gone back to Republicanism; in fact, he referred to himself as a Republican rather than as a Democrat. Jackson stood for the republic of Jefferson and Madison, for a union of proud and powerful states, united yet not obliterated by the national government, encouraged from Washington to thrive and burgeon yet neither bullied nor cosseted by federal bureaucrats.

It was a view Jackson's antagonists could also appreciate. Thurlow Weed was doubtless sincere in opposing the revised New York constitution of 1821 because he "dreaded the effect of extending and cheapening suffrage. . . . I had great veneration for the opinions of Mr. Jefferson, and believing with him that large cities are 'ulcers on the body politic,' I feared . . . that universal suffrage would occasion political demoralization, and ultimately overthrow our government." It was as legitimate a reading of Jeffersonian "democracy," in some respects, as that proffered by Jacksonians. In another instance of the confusion of "conservatism" and "democracy," a far more patriarchal anti-Jacksonian—Rufus King, an "old-Federalist" senator from New York—agreed with Jacksonian "conservative" protests which were also "democratic" recommendations. In a debate of 1824 over the congressional caucus system, he and the Jackson men alike condemned it as a new, insidious device, while defenders of the system pleaded that it was time-hallowed and inherently "democratic," since by its aid the Republicans had once succeeded in vanquishing the Federalists.

The ambivalent character of the Jacksonian movement is illustrated in the prolonged battle over the Bank of the United States. Historians still dispute the exact nature of the affair. However, most believe that after a shaky start in 1817 the Bank, under the direction of Langdon Cheves and then of Nicholas Biddle, performed a useful central banking function. Its activities during the 1820's were shrewd, and they contributed to the establishment of a reasonably sound currency. Later, when Biddle became involved in a feud with Jackson, his tactics were less intelligent, and his attempts to use the B.U.S. as a means of punishing his critics were reckless. But the Bank that Jackson determined to attack was a well-conducted institution.

Not so in Andrew Jackson's eyes. To him, worthy citizens were either planters, farmers, mechanics, or laborers. They produced the only true wealth of the nation. Their product was tangible. The "money power," by contrast, speculated with other men's earnings, and this money was often not even specie but mere paper currency. So to Jackson all banks were suspect as citadels of the "money power." The B.U.S. was worst of all, for it was in his opinion a huge octopus, reaching out through its branches to strangle legitimate enterprise.

The events of the Bank War are too involved to record here. For us the principal features are that Jackson's attitude was naïve, to say the least; that in destroying the B.U.S., first by vetoing its recharter in 1832 and then by withdrawing federal deposits in 1833, he unwittingly assisted in producing a severe depression in 1837; that some of his vociferous allies in the struggle were representatives of state banks, jealous of the position of the B.U.S., or men annoyed by its cautious credit policy but not at all opposed to the "money power" as they interpreted it; and, finally and above all, that Jackson on this particular issue behaved like the sternest, most antique, most superannuated of Republicans, yet managed to win, partly because of his own extraordinary will power, partly because Arcadia rallied to his battle cry, and partly because segments of business enterprise also joined him—though out of very mixed motives.

Conservatism and Democracy

At the beginning of the chapter one composite, conventional version of the origins of American democracy was summarized. According to this version there was a real struggle between west and east, debtor and creditor, self-made and well-born, culminating in the dramatic victories of Andrew Jackson from Tennessee. But according to another version or series of versions which have been summarized in turn, the conventional account is much *too* dramatic. America, to judge from some recent historical interpretations, was torn by no genuine struggles during the period—at least, not over democracy. That development had been insured, by steady, gradual stages, well before 1789. The reforms brought in during the next half-century added to the picture but did not transform it. Jacksonian rhetoric, like that of Jeffersonianism, conjured up half-imaginary villains—"monarchists," "aristocrats," "speculators"—which it then slaughtered in pantomime. In the actual political and social situation they either did not exist or were just as likely to be enlisted on the side of the self-proclaimed heroes.

The first version clearly requires modification. It is likewise obvious that the terms "conservatism" and "democracy," whatever their theoretical opposition, shade into and modify one another as soon as one tries to apply them to anything less elementary than some rough prescription for social equality and political rights. But is the second version entirely acceptable? Granting it a considerable measure of accuracy, it still seems not to provide the whole truth. We have to be on guard against our own generation's historiographical preference for methodology rather than ideology, for studying the blunders or intrigues of past history rather than its underlying ideals. There is another danger in using a word such as "democracy," with all it now conveys of what is obviously, rightly, and inevitably American, and applying it to a bygone era when its connotations were otherwise. We must reckon with the possibility that, whatever historians say about the era from Washington to Jackson, Americans alive at the time may have seen things differently. Deprived of the advantage of hindsight, they may not have realized that the quarrels and problems in which they were immersed could all be explained away as mere myths and subterfuges.

In November, 1828, just after Jackson's victory in the presidential election, a fellow-Tennesseean, General Edmund P. Gaines, wrote to congratulate him. "Your triumph," said Gaines, "is complete—and it is truly a triumph of the great principle of self-government, over the intrigues of aristocracy." Within two years Gaines's enthusiasm for Andrew Jackson had evaporated. Are we to conclude that his initial highflown language was only rhetoric, because he expected patronage and promotion from Jackson? Are personal antipathies the key to the period? Or should we assume that Gaines really meant what he wrote, despite his later disillusionment?

Perhaps a third version of democracy's evolution can be suggested—a version embodying some features from each of the other two. There is some common ground in all interpretations. All historians would concede that, in comparison with Europe, the United States was a relatively classless society. European visitors stressed this. Both Tocqueville and Francis Grund, for example, noted that domestic servants avoided the stigma of that word by being described as "help" (they had actually been known as "help," at least in New England, since the seventeenth century). Americans who traveled in Europe made the same discovery in reverse, as we can see from James

Conservatism and Democracy

Fenimore Cooper's *Notions of the Americans* (1828). There was general agreement that America differed socially from Europe. Children in the United States stood less in awe of their parents, young women there went unchaperoned. The incidental references to America in such a novel as Stendhal's *Le Rouge et le noir* (1830) reveal that Europeans who had never been in the United States took these differences for granted.

The prohibition of titles written into the Constitution, and the disparaging comment on that hereditary, ex-officers' association, the Society of the Cincinnati, testify that from the beginning Americans were determined not to create an aristocracy or the conditions for a monarchy. A decision made in 1792 not to have Washington's head on the coinage—at least not while he was still alive—was part of the same deliberate egalitarianism.

Moreover, the conditions of American life militated against aristocracy. For one reason or another, the vast land grants of the eighteenth century proved to be chimerical. Sizable fortunes were made, but not astronomical fortunes and not static fortunes. Wealth flowed out as well as in. There was surprisingly little permanence. The Astors were long to retain the affluence created by the founder of their dynasty, John Jacob Astor, with his fur-trading empire. But they were exceptional. In general, families did not establish themselves on large estates, and if they did, such stagnation was usually fatal in financial terms. Money constituted the only aristocracy, and money disappeared if treated with true aristocratic disdain. Even in the South, where landholding was equated with gentility, acres were not often held long enough to become ancestral. There was far more buying and selling of property

than one might gather from the region's retrospective mythology, and in the older southern states those who held on
to family plantations found their piety an expensive virtue.
The depleted soil of Virginia could not compete in fertility
with the Mississippi bottomlands. There were families, north
and south, that flourished through several generations. But
often the "dynasty" was over before it was properly established. Consider the fate of all the first presidential families
except the Adamses. Washington died a rich man, at least in
common repute, yet childless, and none of his heirs was able
to turn Mount Vernon to profit except by selling it as a national shrine. Within a few years of Jefferson's death, his handsome home at Monticello was a near ruin. Madison and Monroe
were poor and unable to hand on their name in eminence.

On another point we can also reach common ground: the
fluidity of American politics and the absence of enduring
identity between policy and party. No parliamentary system
is lacking in complexity. British politics in the same period
were complicated enough; Whig and Tory by no means stood
for distinct and fundamentally different doctrines. On occasion the parties in Britain were capable of sudden switches.
In 1845 Sir Robert Peel, the Tory leader, was to reverse his
views on the Corn Laws; in Disraeli's famous words, "the
right honorable gentleman caught the Whigs bathing and
walked away with their clothes." But American politics were
immeasurably more flexible. What was for Peel an agonizing
decision might have been for an American politician almost
a standard maneuver. Disraeli's witticism could fit a score of
American political gambits within a single generation. At the
very beginning of the period there had been lively competition
for and appropriation of those useful party labels "Federalism"

and "Republicanism," each of which acquired a reversed meaning. Later the "Whigs" assumed their name for its patriotic, liberal tone, seeking to impart the stigma of "Toryism" to the Jackson Democrats. What was true of labels was true of policies. Such machinations had an element of opportunism, naturally, but they also point to an effort to resolve the antagonisms and contradictions of America into a manageable formula. And yet they would never have been attempted if the gulf between the parties had been impassably wide.

There is likewise something to be said for and against both versions of the origins of American democracy on the subject of the Federalist party. It seems undeniable that, to a marked degree during the 1790's and to a lesser extent in subsequent years, Federalism *did* represent an element of social, political, and economic privilege which Republicanism deprecated. The most influential of the men who adhered to Federalist doctrines *were* ready to acknowledge themselves as "gentlemen," with a fairly precise satisfaction in doing so, and to withhold the designation from their opponents. In dress, manner, mode of speech, and choice of profession, they formed a quite coherent group, and a group whose beliefs did not accord with the ideology of the common man which was to triumph so signally in nineteenth-century America. Whether Presbyterian clergymen in New England (or Episcopalians in some other state) or merchants and lawyers in New York or Philadelphia, they agreed in broad social attitudes. (Members of the medical profession, though, apparently tended to be Republicans.) Society contained its natural orders; master and servant each had his place and should know that place; the experienced and prosperous should govern; and the inexperienced and unwealthy should accept the dispensation. By and large the "best" society was to be found in the cities of the seaboard. The frontier regions were considered somewhat barbarous.

Such men and such beliefs were numerous in early republican America. For example, they dominated the leading educational institutions. Harvard, Yale, and Columbia were all Federalist. In 1804 Harvard even offered its presidency to the prominent Federalist Fisher Ames, though he would have been the first non-clergyman to hold the office. Ames and his Federalist associates did not approve of any program that would seek to confer complete equality upon mankind. One may find slighting references to "democracy" in the works of any of the leading Federalists. Among the last letters he ever wrote, Alexander Hamilton speaks of democracy as America's worst "disease."

But here a caution is needed. In their usage, as that sturdy patriot and Federalist Noah Webster emphasized, "democracy" was a term derived from Aristotle and other political philosophers to define a perversion of government, a method of rule by mob which was of itself anarchic and unworkable. "Democracy" in this, the accepted meaning, was an invitation to disaster. Federalists like Ames or his Massachusetts colleagues George Cabot and Harrison Gray Otis, or Charles Biddle of Philadelphia, were not selfish "aristocrats" (as their enemies contended) for wishing to preserve some measure of stability. Indeed, in the 1790's their insistence upon stability may have been a godsend for the young republic. The Alien and Sedition Acts of 1798 were, it is true, ill-natured and ill-considered. Yet to judge from similar efforts throughout American history to limit freedom of debate in the name of emergency, they were not uniquely Federalist in character;

and in any case the Federalists paid heavily for this particular blunder.

In short, the Federalists were men of their time, arguing out of a reasonable mixture of conviction and self-interest. The catechism of one of the Washington Benevolent Societies (a Federalist organization) asked potential members: "Are you willing to use your exertion to preserve [America] against the inroads of despotism, monarchy, aristocracy, and democracy?" Except for the equivocal word "democracy," it could have served perfectly well as a Republican ritual. That Federalist views were not hopelessly "reactionary" is suggested too by the fact that the English chemist and radical, Joseph Priestley, an ardent Jeffersonian who came to America in 1794, defended the Constitution in 1803 on what would now be regarded as decidedly "conservative" grounds. He approved of its restraints and even recommended a three-year term (instead of two) for the House of Representatives, so as to remove its members a little further from the restless, ill-informed public. Like the Federalists, or like John Locke, Priestley (who had once had his house wrecked by an English mob) saw nothing wicked in the protection of property. It was a precious right and, to judge from world history, a frail one.

Not all Federalists were rich men or "High-Federalist" in sentiment. Hamilton's doctrines dismayed some of his party. John Adams' ideas on banking, for instance, were closer to those of Jackson than of Hamilton. Many a small farmer in upstate New England, or in western Pennsylvania or Virginia, was a Federalist not from any kind of aristocratic conviction but on quite other "conservative" grounds. He might be a Federalist because he liked the Constitution or venerated

The Nation Takes Shape

George Washington, or because he was shocked by what he took to be the irreligious, immoral nature of Republicanism.

Nevertheless, High-Federalism and Jeffersonian Republicanism were at odds. Federalism gave way gradually and reluctantly. It did not collapse at any one time or place; the political debacle of 1800 is to be attributed largely to John Adams' uncomfortable relations with the Hamiltonians in his party, and to the split within the Federalist ranks over foreign policy. From the outset Federalism was somewhat on the defensive. When Washington consulted Hamilton in 1789 about the presidential style he should maintain, Hamilton replied:

Men's minds are prepared for a pretty high tone in the demeanor of the executive, but I doubt whether for so high a one as in the abstract might be desirable. *The notions of equality are ... too general and too strong* to admit of such a distance being placed between the President and other branches of the government as might even be consistent with a due proportion. [Italics added.]

Hamilton grudged the admission, but he made it. Thenceforward, Federalism was never quite in command of the American situation. Economic opportunity swiftly widened. Political power lay waiting to be seized by whoever could most artfully appeal to the ordinary man; the extension of the franchise was a secondary matter, an obeisance to a principle already acknowledged. As the habit of social deference waned, the Federalists lost touch and lost hold. By their very nature they could not themselves make the appeal—at least not to America as a whole, though they might command support in some areas. In vain to refute the accusation that they were "aristocrats," in vain to countercharge that Jefferson and his men were "radicals" and "atheists." What they advocated in effect was representative democracy, and the duty of the representative was not to cajole his constituents but to interpret their needs according to his own information and conscience. It was impossible to explain such a notion in face of the philanthropic oratory of Republican foes.

Federalist authority failed in politics as in social intercourse. The year 1815 was one of the stages in the process. Discredited by opposition to the war, their gloomy forecasts seemingly disproved by the victory at New Orleans, the Federalists were left without a convincing case. In Europe the peace of 1815 ushered in a time of conservative repression, when monarchies were restored and *ancien régime* statesmen, full of cautionary tales from recent French history, sought to kill the revolutionary virus. Not so in America, which had got over its worst revolutionary excitements nearly twenty years before. In the New World, society continued to develop as hitherto, without a jolt.

So "democracy" came in apace. Chancellor James Kent, the distinguished New York Federalist, did his best during the state constitutional convention of 1821 to condemn the proposal to widen the franchise. He deplored the "disposition to vibrate from a well-balanced government to the extremes of the democratic doctrines" and claimed that ten years previously such a proposal "would have struck the public mind with astonishment and terror. So rapid has been the career of our vibration." Possibly, but it no longer had much impact; the measure was carried.

In Connecticut, according to Samuel Goodrich, the trend had existed for some years but was confirmed in 1818. One token was the change in apparel:

Powder and queues, cocked-hats and broad-brims, white-top boots, breeches, and shoe-buckles—signs and symbols of a generation, a few examples of which still lingered among us—finally departed with the Charter of Charles II, while with the new constitution of 1818, short hair, pantaloons, and round hats with narrow brims, became the established costume of men of all classes.

The evolution of "democracy" was not simple. As we have noted, each successive Republican administration after the Federalist downfall of 1800 took on more and more of the programs of "conservatism," while the judiciary in general and the Supreme Court in particular abided by and propagated Federalist doctrine. When we return to the problem of defining "democracy," other difficulties arise. Thus, in the American novel as practiced by James Fenimore Cooper and long afterward, quite sharp class demarcations are taken for granted. One hypothesis is that American novelists were conservative by temperament. But this seems dubious, even if we amend it to suggest that without a conflict the novelist has no plot, that class conflict is a classic theme for fiction, and that the American novelist inherited a literary tradition which did not conform to the actualities of the American scene.

It seems more satisfactory to assume that novels are a fairly accurate gauge of social mores, that class distinctions had existed and continued to exist in the United States, but that such distinctions, in comparison with those of Europe, were minor and fluid.

We may also argue that the common-man rhetoric, while not literally descriptive of American conditions, was a powerful force toward producing full "democracy." In certain areas, notably in politics, it was all-powerful. The rhetoric was coupled, however, with an element of actual conservatism. This is in part to be understood as a survival of older mores. Conservatism was also institutionalized in certain professions.

Conservatism and Democracy

The law was one, to some extent. A better example could be found in the regular army and navy—hierarchical subsocieties whose officers held sharply aloof from the enlisted men. The institutions embodying the values of these professions—West Point or the federal courts or even to a degree the Senate—had considerable power to mold men in a "conservative" image.

The South is another "conservative" case, since it resisted many of the implications of democracy. However, in a variety of ways the South too, especially in the newer states, represented a remarkably open and egalitarian society, once we put aside the fact of slavery and the romantic legends of aristocratic plantation life.

In the North too, "conservative" features could be identified. The America of Jackson's day was in certain senses less "democratic" than that of Washington's, or at any rate more self-conscious. By then there were some mercantile fortunes, factories, city poor, raw immigrants, awakenings of trade unionism. The symptoms of unrest are trifling in comparison with the "two nations" of Chartist England in the same epoch and far removed in spirit from the New Deal radicalism of the United States a century later. Yet they are a factor to include in the blurred and complex balance sheet of democracy-conservatism.

In the eyes of intelligent Federalists like Harrison Gray Otis, or of a disillusioned Democrat like Fenimore Cooper in the 1830's, the coronation of the common man *was* epitomized in the election of Andrew Jackson, and it was something of a disaster for America. Addressing the hero of his novel *Homeward Bound* (1838), Cooper cries: "You have been dreaming abroad [in Europe] . . . while your country has retrograded, in all that is respectable and good, a century in a dozen years."

The Nation Takes Shape

"Whole hog" democracy, as distinct from the "qualified" democracy preferred by Federalists, entailed—they alleged—a great deal of cant, demagogism, vulgarity. The "common man" was grossly flattered. Education, experience, seniority, and other sober merits were falsely decried, xenophobia and complacent ignorance encouraged.

The deterioration was evident, Federalists thought, in the quality of American leadership. Politics became extraordinarily important to Americans. According to European visitors, it was what they talked about in lieu of literature or the arts. It was, one might say, all things to all men: means to power, means to wealth, means of amusement. In this arena, men with the stiff rectitude of a Washington or an Adams were increasingly at a disadvantage. Perhaps their appearance in the first place had been a unique circumstance, the result of the special, ennobling crisis of independence. In any event, they gave way to the horde of politicians. There were still talent, intelligence, integrity in Congress and—more rarely—in state legislatures. But such virtues were less frequent and too often touched with venality (Daniel Webster), distorted by sectional pride (John C. Calhoun), or warped by presidential ambition (Henry Clay).

These men were among the ablest. There was remarkable quality in Andrew Jackson, too, or in Benton and a score of other congressmen. But at the lower levels the spectacle was less impressive. During these years, America's richly cynical vocabulary of politics was being formed. *Niles' Register* said in 1823 that the word "politician" in its revised meaning applied to "persons who have little if any regard for the welfare of the republic unless as immediately connected with . . . their own private pursuits." Ninian Edwards in 1812 spoke of "logrolling"—originally a method by which backwoodsmen assisted one another—as a Kentucky expression for political bargaining. The Gerrymander was invented in Massachusetts in 1812, under the governorship of Elbridge Gerry, as a method of redrawing electoral boundaries "for the sake of economizing majorities." The word "lobby-agent" and its shorter form "lobbyist" were commonly used as early as 1832. The adjective "noncommittal," according to Thurlow Weed, was applied initially to Van Buren, a politician who "had the sagacity at an early date to discover the danger of opposing himself to a strong current of public sentiment."

This was the flavor of American democracy—a little specious, a little corrupt, redolent of the hustings and the Fourth of July oration, apt to confuse equality with crass mediocrity. Or so an old-guard Federalist was entitled to maintain. What he and his kind did not grasp (Tocqueville was the first to do so with philosophical detachment) was that America properly speaking had no choice. The past weighed with her in 1789 and thereafter. Yet alone among modern nations, in another sense, she had a genuine freedom to choose. The range of choice, though never as wide as Federalists and Republicans believed (or chose to argue), was appreciable: hence the uproar of the 1790's. Her choice lay between "whole hog" and "qualified" democracy. Both would have their drawbacks— the latter in the shape of subtle forms of snobbery, rule by complacent elites, codes of privilege, discrimination against creed and surname.

Neither alternative was ideal, and Jacksonian Democracy can be convicted of doing the wrong thing for the right reason as well as the right thing for the wrong reason. The persistence of Negro slavery was a tragic violation of the professed American creed. But on the whole the road taken was the appropriate road for America. The political and other manifestations were all concomitant; better perhaps the contempt for "book-learning," the use of cuspidor and whittling knife, the ebullient jobbery of Congress, than the icy affronts of European society at its worst, the savage hatreds underneath. The more perceptive Federalists gradually understood. They knew that the rhetoric, the lay of the land, the likely solution of the American equation all moved away from them. Being Americans, it did not take most of them long to join what they could not hope to defeat.

VIII

The American Character

In summing up the quality of the period 1789–1837 two temptations should be avoided. One is that of investing it with a false aura of tranquillity. In some respects, especially up to 1815, it was a time of prolonged crisis, full of regret and foreboding, hostility and confusion. The other danger is of assuming that the period constitutes an "era" of its own, separate from what came before and after, instead of being merely a half-century removed from the continuum of American history.

There is nevertheless some point in regarding the period as an entity and in trying to identify its special features. After all, its terminal dates have a certain force. At least 1789 has, as the beginning of the United States under a new Constitution. The working-out of that Constitution, in its various governmental, judicial, political, economic, social, and patriotic implications, is in large part the story of the period. As for 1837, it or its near neighbors in the decade of the 1830's can be argued to mark the inauguration of another era.

The Nation Takes Shape

Some of these events are perhaps trivial, or at any rate superficial in the exact sense of the word. Thus in 1837 the young writer Nathaniel Hawthorne notes that a new fashion, imported from England, has appeared among American naval officers of his own age: they have started to sport mustaches. Goatees and other shapes of beard come in soon after; the masculine face of the succeeding generation—including Hawthorne's—will look different. So, by degrees, will the nation's architecture, though the classical revival maintains its popularity for some while. In 1836 the architects Town and Davis design New York University, in Washington Square, as a Gothic creation; it is anticipated by other Gothic structures, some a generation old, yet still unlike the porticoed and pedimented official or commercial buildings that Americans have grown accustomed to.

There are technological changes: 1835 is the year in which Samuel Colt patents the revolver, 1836 the moment when Samuel F. B. Morse applies for a patent on his telegraph (though he did not get it or transmit the famous message, "What hath God wrought," in Morse code until 1844). Cyrus H. McCormick takes out a patent on his reaper in 1834. John Deere introduces the steel plow in 1837; other agricultural inventors produce the crude prototype of the threshing machine. Charles Goodyear manages to vulcanize rubber in 1839.

There are social-intellectual indicators. The first women's college in the United States, Mount Holyoke Seminary, opens its doors in 1837 (Oberlin College, in Ohio, had taken the pioneer step of becoming coeducational in 1833). Eighteen thirty-seven is the year of Ralph Waldo Emerson's "American Scholar" address to the Phi Beta Kappa Society of Harvard, not the first or the last, yet one of the most eloquent of Amer-

The American Character

ica's declarations of cultural independence. The same year sees the foundation of the American Temperance Society; this is the period of ambitious efforts to combat drunkenness. The 1830's are the decade of the *Book of Mormon* and of the bitterly opposed emergence of the Latter-day Saints—to be followed by other religious and communitarian movements.

About the same time there are the first signs of American "nativism" in the face of Irish-Catholic immigration: some anti-Irish disturbances in Boston, the publication of such scurrilous anti-Catholic literature as *The Awful Disclosures of Maria Monk*. Party politics acquire a new emphasis with the birth of the Whig organization in 1834. There are other incidents of ominous import. The first attempt—a botched one—to assassinate an American President (in this case Andrew Jackson) is made in 1835. During the decade the sectional dispute over slavery begins to be aggravated. Its symptoms include the founding of William Lloyd Garrison's abolitionist magazine the *Liberator* in Boston and the Nat Turner slave insurrection in Virginia (both in 1831), the establishment (1833) of the American Antislavery Society, the suppression of antislavery petitions in Congress by the "gag rules" of 1836, and the murder in Illinois (1837) of the abolitionist Elijah P. Lovejoy.

There does seem a rough validity to the notion of the 1830's as some sort of watershed in American history. What lies between it and the earlier watershed of 1789 may be thought to possess a kind of unity.

In one respect the period can be characterized as "formative." During this half-century the precedents are made and set. The rules and usages of government, the areas of authority and controversy between executive and legislative or federal and state systems, the alignments of party politics, the assumptions of foreign policy, the patterns of land settlement, the conditions of economic growth, the symbols of nationalism, and the weapons of sectionalism: all these have their origins and acquire a measure of finality within the period.

In other respects the period can be described as "premodern." With the partial exception of Andrew Jackson, its presidents reveal personalities quite unlike those of Martin Van Buren and his successors. Its men of letters—from the two giants, Washington Irving and James Fenimore Cooper, down to the minor scribblers and sermonizers—have a different tone from those of the next generation. Emerson was a little unjust to his father's Massachusetts when he said that from 1790 to 1820 there was not a book, poem, conversation, or thought in the whole state. But there is no denying the change of atmosphere that led successively from Congregationalism through Unitarianism to the later fervors of Transcendentalism. A Whitman or Melville, or an Edgar Allan Poe, could not be accommodated within the literary milieux of the United States much before 1837. The educational and cultural institutions of the country are in general staid, restricted, gentlemanly in outlook. College curriculums, as well as the format and contents of periodicals like the *North American Review*, have a European cast. There is a new device for adult education in the shape of the lyceum movement, but the idea was imported from England.

One way of putting this is to say that America during the half-century is still quasi-colonial in status. The United States is premodern in not having achieved truly national status. But her belief that she will achieve it, and thereby achieve a character utterly separate from that of Europe, is much stronger than in later times—when it actually has more justification. Hence, it could be argued, a duality in the American attitude to Europe which is later modified. The United States is more thoroughly obligated to, more overawed by, Europe. Europe, Britain in particular, is the great fount of learning, art, industry, and wealth. Bishop Philander Chase of Ohio, in England during 1823–24 on a fund-raising expedition, has no embarrassment and no difficulty in collecting $30,000 there to found Kenyon College as an Episcopalian missionary outpost. But the United States is moralistically certain that she must not and need not follow suit in the wicked examples set by Europe. In this pre-industrial era there is a surprising unanimity in the horror with which Americans, whatever their region or profession, view the black squalor of Britain's manufacturing areas. The pall of soot has not yet descended on the New World, the industrial slums are not yet built. Arcadia is still, if half a dream, half real also:

> Here something still like Eden looks;
> Honey in woods, juleps in brooks.

Other moralities are likewise more or less intact. In this period before the onset of large-scale immigration, the population is relatively homogeneous. The word "immigrant" is apparently of American coinage, dating back to about 1789. But the concept of free immigration, as something to defend or to query according to whether it is viewed as a principle of true Americanism or as a threat to America's ethnic purity, is not yet in serious dispute. By the 1830's sectional emotions are becoming intense. But the full uproar is reserved to the next generation. Until the last decade of the half-century, slave emancipation societies are more common in the South than in the North. Under the various state schemes of gradual emancipation, slavery exists legally in such northern states as New York and New Jersey well into the nineteenth century. Many prominent men, Madison, Monroe, and John Marshall among them, reach provisional agreement on the solution of sending the slaves back as free men to Africa. This is the program of the American Colonization Society (founded in 1817), and this the origin of the independent republic of Liberia, whose capital, Monrovia, is named in tribute to the American President of the time. Slavery is acknowledged to be a dreadful problem, but at least one that can be discussed without excessive rancor until the changing mood of the 1830's.

Finally, the period is in some ways pre-expansionist. Within it, the national domain is enormously enlarged. Indian tribes are dispossessed of millions of acres; this is par excellence the time of Indian treaties, Indian removals. But it is not yet quite the era of Manifest Destiny, though that will come in a decade. The civilizing and settling mission of the United States is not yet quite projected into a providential duty to occupy the entire subcontinent.

This much said, the theme of America as "premodern" from 1789 to 1837 ought not to be pushed too far. Granted that there are some features of the time that disappear subsequently—its homogeneity of population and its pre-industrial economy are two of the chief examples—nevertheless, the American character seems to have been formed in essence within a generation of George Washington's accession to the presidency. How else are we to account for the remarkable freshness, even for the present day, of Alexis de Tocqueville's *Democracy in America*, which was based on a visit to the United States in

The American Character

1831–32? "National character" is a hazy expression. But for our approximate purposes we may think of it as an assemblage of beliefs and patterns of behavior which are widely recognized, inside and outside the country in question, as being more common among its citizens than among those of other nations. If this clumsy description is acceptable, then we may go on to suggest that Tocqueville's diagnosis of American attitudes to commerce, to social class, to politics, to literature, and a dozen other matters could be applied with surprising relevance to the America of 1870 or even 1950.

One might object that Tocqueville was not really writing about the United States but about the social and political phenomenon of democracy, and that his book is therefore not a guide to American character but a brilliant piece of intellectual prophecy relating to the whole Western world. The criticism cannot be altogether brushed aside. Now and then, in the interests of his thesis, he did overstress the "democratic" ethos of America and the correspondingly "aristocratic" nature of Europe, making the one stand schematically for tomorrow and the other for yesterday. However, the objection can be answered in large part by pointing out that Tocqueville's diary of his American travels—a day-to-day record—embodies the same observations. So, broadly speaking, do the travel narratives of other contemporary European visitors, and so do the commentaries by Americans of the period when they discuss their native qualities. Then, as now, the South was held to be an exception to the prevailing American mood of egalitarian bustle. Then, as now, the more recently settled western areas were praised by some witnesses for their additional informality or "democracy" and criticized by others for their excessive uncouthness. But on the whole, whether favorable or not, the picture drawn by Tocqueville and by lesser men was consistent and is still recognizable.

To give an example, not until 1837 did Washington Irving coin an expression that gained wide currency, when he wrote of "the Almighty Dollar, that great object of universal devotion throughout our land." The phrase was picked up and given wider circulation by Charles Dickens in his *American Notes* (1840). Might it be classified among the items listed above that mark the beginning of another era, one more wholeheartedly devoted to commerce and industry? No, for there are earlier examples of the same opinion. The Irish poet Thomas Moore, touring America in 1804, wrote:

> Long has the love of gold, that meanest rage,
> And latest folly of man's sinking age . . .
> Long has it palsied every grasping hand
> And greedy spirit through this bartering land.

Disregard Moore as too rabidly hostile to be reliable; his accusation is nevertheless supported by Daniel Webster, who in an oration of 1809 on "The State of Our Literature" attributed America's cultural mediocrity to the nation's "grovelling . . . propensity" to gold. The same charge is leveled even before the Revolution by the Pennsylvania poet Nathaniel Evans:

> And we are in a climate cast
> Where few the muse can relish
>   Where all the doctrine now that's told
>   Is that a shining heap of gold
> Alone can man embellish.

In other contexts, these complaints appear as causes for congratulation, or at any rate as distinctive and defensible elements in the American makeup. The United States, that is, tends to a money standard of value and achievement because she is free from the hereditary subserviences of Europe. In her socially and geographically mobile society, the race *is* to the swift and the battle to the strong. The rewards are great in a situation where to the inheritance of European skill and capital are added abundant natural resources and an adaptable, quickly "Americanized" or standardized population. Inevitably they are for the most part monetary rewards, since the alternatives—titles, decorations, special privileges—would imply an aristocratic social order of the old European type. Authority and prestige are of course accompanied by financial power in the European context. But they are, by comparison, more permanent, more heritable, more honorific, and less baldly based upon money. Yet the European miser, hoarding and gloating over his gold, has hardly any counterpart in American folklore.

In a new and open social order the fine arts are necessarily at a disadvantage. Poetry, drama, abstract thought, music, painting, sculpture, have traditionally—except for such popular manifestations as the ballad—been the preserve of aristocracy; they are a function of wealth and leisure. America, lacking a leisured upper class and intent on opening up the country, has only a secondary interest in the arts unless they are "useful" arts. The careers of her early painters illustrate the point. Nearly all, from Stuart, West, and Copley onward, go to Europe because the United States provides them neither with advanced instruction in the craft nor with enough patrons to purchase the product. John Trumbull of Connecticut projects a series of patriotic tableaux and finally secures a commission to execute some for Congress, but not until he has learned to his disgust that few private subscribers are forthcoming in the

The Nation Takes Shape

United States. "Connecticut is not Athens!" his father, Governor Jonathan Trumbull, once sharply reminded him. Would-be authors have similar grievances: thus their habit of interpreting the American cash nexus as the lowest of mercenary endeavors. Fulton and Morse, who both set out to be painters, discover that there is little profit and status in the limner's or landscapist's talent. Applied art is more in demand. And so both lay aside their brushes eventually and become inventors.

To observers in the early nineteenth century, then, Americans seem restless, competitive, "go-ahead" (another revealing Americanism coined in Jackson's time), egalitarian, naïve, serious, coarse and importunate yet in some ways prim and moralistic, matter-of-fact and yet imbued with vague, soaring notions of American futurity. This last point was wittily made by Tocqueville, in the comment that the American mind is either concentrated upon the practical and parochial or else diffused in vast and formless reverie, and that in between lies a vacuum. One could go on adding almost indefinitely to the list of American characteristics identified during the period, and nearly all would support the assertion that American "national character" has not altered fundamentally since its early definitions. Similarly, if we glance at the conflicting elements in the picture and at the actual controversies that have separated individual from individual and section from section in American history, there appear to be certain enduring features in the record.

However, as the two previous chapters have indicated, it is extremely difficult to analyze American experience in satisfactory terms. Some Europeans and a few disillusioned Americans during the period 1789–1837 gave up the effort or concluded that the effort was not worth making. The United

States, they felt, was an unstable experiment, hopelessly divided within itself, lacking in all the necessary safeguards of true nationhood, like some badly designed Mississippi steamboat whirling downriver until the irrevocable collision or explosion shattered her. Even Tocqueville, immeasurably more judicious than most spectators, doubted whether the Union could long hold together—and of course it did not.

By contrast, a number of recent American historians have dwelt upon the essential soundness of their country's early disposition. Seizing like Tocqueville on the absence of feudalism as the basic clue to American national development—on the fact that she was "born in broad daylight," unhampered by the past, dating the origin of her own national epic no farther back than 1776 and therefore able to carry the national legend around with her, so to speak, as a portable heritage—seizing on this truth, these historians have interpreted America's past as an organic affair. American politics were to a considerable degree a matter of *ad hoc* local or sectional bargaining. American ideology was an affair of fine shades, qualifications, ambiguities, contradictions. Perhaps, in such a view, it could be held that Emerson came near to grasping a subtle truth. In his unsystematic, perceptive way he typified the American intellect. He may have touched the heart of American reality with his doctrine of "compensation," according to which dualities are friendly rather than inimical, since they cancel one another out and thus lead to a kind of equilibrium:

> Foolish hands may mix and mar;
> Wise and sure the issues are.
> Round they roll till dark is light.

Some of these newer interpretations are highly sophisticated, so much so that they come full circle and are able to make good use of the old cynical-contemptuous, European view of the United States as a mere shapeless agglomerate. Thus they might fasten upon and extract significance from a casual remark made by the British visitor Mrs. Trollope as she watched a Methodist camp meeting in Ohio. The passage as a whole, from her book *Domestic Manners of the Americans* (1832) is censorious. But she also admits, "I . . . experienced a strange vibration between tragic and comic feeling." In such an *aperçu* a modern commentator might find much food for thought, for it hints at the tantalizing oddity of some sides of American history that could mean little or could mean far more than appears at first glimpse. The revivalist frenzy Mrs. Trollope witnesses is cheap, banal, erotic. Yet it has a pathos, a novelty, a colloquial vigor, a directness of emotion that go deeper than the occasion—like that of a Negro spiritual (the word "spiritual" being both neologist noun and poignant adjective).

Between the sweeping disapproval of a Frances Trollope and the refined insights of a study like R. W. B. Lewis' *The American Adam: Innocence, Tragedy, and Tradition in the Nineteenth Century* (1955) come a quantity of attempts to interpret American history in terms of some bold polarity. In the widest terms of all, the division is seen as that of America versus Europe, which can be taken to imply democracy versus aristocracy, adaptability versus rigidity, innocence versus experience, and so on. Or, in the influential thesis of Frederick Jackson Turner, as West versus East, which represents a not-too-different polarity. Some scholars, for instance, now expound American history within an "Atlantic community," within which in turn there is a boundary between West and East—a boundary that shifts steadily inland across America, so that during part of the nineteenth century the eastern seaboard of the United States is linked economically and culturally with Europe rather than with the trans-Appalachian West.

Or again, there is the familiar polarity of Jefferson versus Hamilton, which can be visualized as a contest between Republicanism and Federalism, or agrarianism and capitalism, or rural life and urbanism, or debtor and creditor, or free trade and the tariff, or Jacksonianism and the "Monster Bank," or state rights and centralization in government, or—by extension —North and South, which can be again stylized as a division between Massachusetts and Virginia or between freedom and slavery. Present in some interpretations is a theory of class conflict or of sectional controversy as being principally economic in origin.

There is much to be said for these polarities. They have the merit of clarity. They satisfy our ingrained habit of thinking dualistically, in terms of body and soul, god and devil, and so on; we respond readily, for example, to Emerson's idea of an American schism between "the party of the Past and the party of the Future" or to George Bancroft's statement of an immemorial feud between "the capitalist and laborer, the house of Have and the house of Want." They escape the current tendency in historiography to explain away conflicts as mere smoke screens behind which men maneuver and chaffer for "real" benefits.

The arguments epitomized in the string of contests cited above *were* important to those involved in them. Apart from the slavery dispute, perhaps no American controversy was as implacable as some in Europe. They often seem almost pastorally mild after one has looked at the mortal enmities of the Old World during the period. But though in this sense they might be circumscribed quarrels, some of them implied profound differences of viewpoint on how to shape the future. Americans under their new Constitution were gravely conscious that their decisions would be imprinted upon and enlarged in the lives of successive generations. Theirs, they wished to believe, was *tabula rasa*—the clean slate.

But current historiography has nevertheless made some of these polarities seem blurred and dubious; Americans even more than the rest of mankind have been described as likelier to choose "and . . . and" than "either . . . or." As chapter vii indicates, Republicanism versus Federalism and Jackson versus the B.U.S. are instances of contests that are by no means clear cut. It is not just that we are uncertain which side is hero and which villain, but that we are not always able to say with confidence which side is which, so confusing and sudden are the shifts in allegiance. Moreover, though some of the polarities seem nearly synonymous and though all are to some extent linked with one another, it is not possible to arrange them meaningfully by parceling them into two teams, like this:

America	Europe
West	East
Democracy	Aristocracy
Agrarianism	Capitalism
State Rights	Centralization
South	North

There is a rough correspondence, perhaps, in each of the two groups. But it is so rough as to be almost worthless. Worse than that, it is positively misleading. Overly simple groupings of this kind have led some American historians to attach a spurious dynamism to geography (for such men, one feels, if Bishop Berkeley had never written his celebrated line, "Westward the course of empire," it would have been necessary to invent it. How fitting that the line was stamped on the cover of the first volume of Bancroft's sonorously patriotic history, published in 1834). Others have exaggerated the difference between Europe and the United States, making Europe more tyrannical and obsolescent than it really was and the United States more freedom-loving and progressive than any nation could be under heaven. One can but maintain that Turner's frontier thesis, while "true" and "useful" within limits, suffers from being so simplistic in shape. In his day there were cogent reasons for attempting a synthesis of geography-*cum*-idealism. And in European history, partly because one is dealing with fixed geographical/ethnic areas, partly because of the severity of European controversies and their relation to a well-defined class and occupational structure, it *is* possible to make up quite coherent "teams" of the sort shown above.

For the United States, the thing cannot be done. As some recent neoconservative writings reveal, the teams will not line up properly. What is "South" doing in the left-hand table if "Aristocracy" is in the right-hand column? One cannot construct an American "conservative" or "liberal" genealogy by any straightforward method. The result is full of illegitimacies, adoptions, divorces, remarriages.

If two teams cannot be chosen, is there any other way of representing the issues of American history for the period (which, to reiterate, embodies or foreshadows most of the major problems in American domestic experience)? The word "polarity" suggests a slightly less obvious diagram, by reminding us of a compass. So let us construct a diagram of polarities set out as a kind of compass and using the same twelve labels as before. North, South, East, and West, though standing for states of mind as well as actual geographical areas of the United States,

can be left in their conventional places, as if they were compass points.

This is a more plausible representation. If we regard each of
the twelve "points" as a concept or a cluster of attitudes, then
this diagram suggests better than the two-team listing the complexities of the American situation. In fact, the diagram could
be thought of more fitly as a spectrum of continuous and con-
tinuously modified color, each "point" shading off into those
adjacent. Neighboring attitudes are shown to bear a sympa-

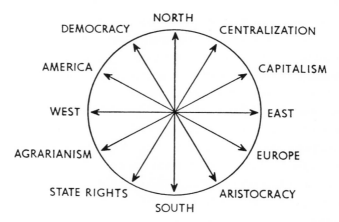

thetic relationship to one another—like that between "centralization" and "capitalism." In fact, so do any four attitudes
within a quadrant—say "aristocracy," "South," "state rights,"
"agrarianism." The polar opposites can be seen as mutually antagonistic. Here is a pictorial representation that avoids some
of the oversimplifications we have alluded to.

However, the diagram is still not really satisfactory, and no
reshuffling of the points will altogether remedy its weaknesses.
One trouble is that it perpetuates the notion that the West is

more innately "American" than the East and that the West is almost diametrically opposed to "capitalism." Also, of course, the diagram is static. It does not take into account the fluctuations of American development: the process, for instance, by which North and West were drawn together, instead of West to South, or that by which "state rights" became a southern instead of a New England doctrine.

Like the effort to compile two rival teams, it overlooks a basic truth about America. This is the truth grasped by Tocqueville, though he missed some of the historical factors that underlay it and though he emphasized the Europe-America polarity a little too much: in comparison with at any rate the Europe of his father's day, the United States was an amazingly unformed and unfettered society. What was already formed, thanks to the British heritage and to the happy outcome of the Revolutionary War, was acquisitive, Protestant, libertarian, reasonably law-abiding. The rest was a matter for posterity to determine or, rather, for the Americans themselves to impose upon posterity, since they were free agents to a unique degree.

In this whole context rather than in preoccupation with the frontier, the United States was differentiated from Europe (though, in relation to the European continent, Britain itself was a more open and flexible society).

This is not to contend that America had no problems during the period or that she solved them. She was haunted by colonialism and wracked with dissension at the same time that she grew and thrived and exulted. But the point to stress, if we are searching for interpretations, is this: There are ideological polarities of real import. The nature and mission of the United States, the struggle to make it in a new likeness without reference to the Old World, constituted a vital quest, and the continuing influence of Europe posed a genuine dilemma. The wrangle over the balance between the federal government and the states, while it later lost much of its gravity, was during the period a weighty matter. The mutual hostilities of North and South embraced profound issues of government, political economy, and human nature.

These are all significant, and so are other issues touched on in preceding chapters. Moreover, Americans alive between 1789 and 1837 took them seriously. But—and here we reach the crux—though the polarities are more or less fixed, the personnel are not. The arguments stand fast, rooted in permanent considerations of law, order, and society, heavy and dignified (if not, as we have seen, speculative in the sense of academic philosophy). The men who employ the arguments, however, constantly change their own standpoints. They change their minds and their political parties, and the parties likewise reverse names and strategies. In 1815 New England and its "godlike" Daniel Webster adopt the extreme state-rights position, while the South and its spokesman John C. Calhoun breathe the spirit of nationalism. Fifteen years later, Calhoun and the South are sectionalist; Webster and his region stand for the federal Union. Similar examples can be found, not merely in politics, throughout the land and throughout the half-century.

Why? Not because politicians were all rogues or because Americans were all vulgar opportunists. But for two reasons. First, that since the United States was inchoate, there were no permanent sectional, political, economic, religious, or occupational groupings of the kind which are immediately recognizable in Europe and which impart a degree of coherence to European affairs even when these affairs include revolutions or other violent upheavals. American society was not entirely fluid; all sorts of rules and associations affected its operation. But they did not form inviolable taboos and imperatives. American society was tentative. Its rules could be modified; "joiners" could be and were "leavers," moving from one societal institution to another at will, and sometimes abruptly from one polar extreme to the other. Such looseness perhaps encouraged cynicism and corruptness of purpose, as permissive situations tend to. But expediency was not an inherent vice.

The second reason has already been suggested. It is that the range of possible choices was, by European standards, extraordinarily wide. Not merely was the American at liberty to change his occupation, his religious and political affiliations, his home and state; he saw before him all sorts of more solemn alternatives on which he was required by the nature of American democracy to have an opinion. His vote was endlessly solicited, his brain teased by conundrums about internal improvements, interstate commerce, the limits of suffrage, policy on land settlement, new states, tariffs. What he decided might make or mar his country. But how on such complex questions *could* he decide? No wonder that the average American changed his mind or did not bother to have an opinion or voted according to calculations of how his pocket would feel—and heavy financial stakes were frequently involved. Again, he was not being inherently irresponsible.

To recapitulate, the polarities are more or less fixed, the personnel are not. The people choose the position that matches their need or conviction of the moment and will shift to another if pressed. Some verities or some symbols of nationality —the Christian church, the Declaration of Independence, the Constitution, the memory of George Washington—are unchallenged in their broad generality; they are in the possession of virtually all Americans. The rest are a common heritage that may be repudiated or accepted as the situation dictates. The comedy of the situation is not lost upon Americans; one side of their nature, in the eyes of European visitors, is a cliché-ridden pomposity that makes them talk all too often like Supreme Court justices or like Independence Day orators. But the other side is a glorious irreverence; they coin big, nonsensical words like "splendiferous," revel in mock solemnity, delight in puncturing the national self-image, for the disparity between the unchanging pieties of nationhood and the nimble uses to which they are put is rich material for the humorist.

A diagram that sought to convey something of this would be too complicated to depict here. In part, though, it could still be conceived of as a fixed compass card of concept polarities, except that we might remove the four geographical labels—North, South, East, West—from the card and perhaps substitute other polarities. On top of the fixed card we might visualize another, floating dial. The superimposed dial would represent various sectional, political, and occupational groups pivoted loosely above the permanent card, defining positions in relation to it: a dial fluctuating, swayed, so cynical-righteous that Tocqueville shuddered a little at the intellectual slovenliness of America, so unsteady that he foresaw the dismemberment of the Union, so buoyant that he rightly marveled at the fortuitous miracle of American democracy.

Such a device may serve to elucidate much that is characteristic and puzzling in American experience. From George Washington to Andrew Jackson (and since), it is the symbol of a people at once erratic and straightforward, self-conscious and demonstrative, friendly and suspicious, tolerant and bigoted, radical and conservative, confident and nostalgic. "Inconsistencies cannot both be right," says the philosopher Imlac in Samuel Johnson's *Rasselas;* "but, imputed to man, they may both be true." His comment hints that one might enter similar claims on behalf of other peoples. Even so, as the events of the formative half-century from 1789 to 1837 may have made plain, it is no accident that while the American language abounds in such words and expressions as "footloose" and "every which way," many of America's national and state mottoes emphasize unity, sameness, perpetuity. Not all these expressions and mottoes were coined during the period but nearly all were anticipated then.

Bibliographical Note

Lack of space, as well as of expert knowledge, has prevented me from exploring a number of fascinating topics. I have tried to select those that seemed of greatest significance, though aware that my choice and my views would not coincide with everyone else's.

In this brief bibliographical appendage to a brief book I wish to draw the reader's attention to works—particularly newer ones—that will take him further than I have gone, and not necessarily in the same direction. I assume that he will already have within reach such indispensable works of reference as Samuel F. Bemis and Grace G. Griffin, *Guide to the Diplomatic History of the United States, 1775–1921* (1935); Oscar Handlin *et al.*, *Harvard Guide to American History* (1954); James D. Hart, *Oxford Companion to American Literature* (3d ed., 1956); and Richard B. Morris, *Encyclopedia of American History* (1953). I have also often consulted Mitford M. Mathews' *Dictionary of Americanisms* (1-vol. ed., 1956).

Among general surveys of the period the most ambitious and most distinguished is still that by Henry Adams, *History of the United States during the Administrations of Thomas Jefferson and James Madison* (9 vols., 1889–91). It is also available in an abridged edition in two volumes under the title *The Formative Years* (1948). Nathan Schachner's *The Founding Fathers* (1954) provides a useful prelude, since it deals with the administrations of George Washington and John Adams. George Dangerfield's *The Era of Good Feel-*

ings (1953), an intelligent narrative of the political transition of American democracy from the War of 1812 to the election of Andrew Jackson, is another valuable supplement. The social history of the period is covered by John A. Krout and Dixon R. Fox in *The Completion of Independence, 1790–1830* (1944), one of the "History of American Life" series, and in Gaillard Hunt, *Life in America One Hundred Years Ago* (1914). Its cultural atmosphere is evoked in Van Wyck Brooks's *The World of Washington Irving* (1944). See also Merle Curti, *The Growth of American Thought* (2d ed., 1951), and Joseph Dorfman, *The Economic Mind in American Civilization* (2 vols., 1946).

There are three pioneering volumes by Leonard D. White on the administrative operations and personnel of the federal government: *The Federalists, 1789–1801* (1948), *The Jeffersonians, 1801–1829* (1951), and *The Jacksonians, 1829–1861* (1954). William O. Lynch's *Fifty Years of Party Warfare, 1789–1837* (1931) is a detailed though uneven guide to political controversy. Legal and constitutional problems are clearly summarized in Homer C. Hockett's *The Constitutional History of the United States, 1776–1826* (1939) and with more particular emphasis in Charles G. Haines's *The Role of the Supreme Court in American Government and Politics, 1789–1835* (1944). J. H. Powell's *The Books of a New Nation: United States Government Publications, 1774–1814* (1957) illustrates within a special sphere the difficulties of initiating a new government. And see W. B. Bryan, *A History of the National Capital* (2 vols., 1914–16); Mary L. Hinsdale, *A History of the President's Cabinet* (1911); and Norman J. Small, *Some Presidential Interpretation of the Presidency* (1932).

Biography should not be overlooked. The fullest, though still not an entirely satisfactory, treatment of Washington's presidency is to be found in Volume VI of Douglas Southall Freeman's majestic work, *George Washington: A Biography*, subtitled *Patriot and President, 1784–1793* (1954), and in the seventh volume, *First in Peace, 1793–1799* (1957), by Freeman's associates John Alexander Carroll and Mary Wells Ashworth. The briefest recent interpretation is Marcus Cunliffe's *George Washington: Man and Monument* (1958). Nathan Schachner has written competent lives of *Alexander Hamilton* (1946; reprinted 1957) and *Thomas Jefferson* (2 vols., 1951; reprinted in 1, 1957). *John Jay: Defender of Liberty* (1935) is a readable work by Frank Monaghan. Irving Brant's successive volumes on

The Nation Takes Shape

James Madison (*Father of the Constitution, 1787–1800* [1950]; *Secretary of State, 1800–1809* [1953]; *The President, 1809–1812* [1956]) make a powerful plea for their subject, especially for his conduct as President—for which, Brant maintains, he was unfairly condemned by Federalist contemporaries and by subsequent historians, including Henry Adams.

On foreign policy one of the best recent monographs is Bradford Perkins' *The First Rapprochement: England and the United States, 1795–1805* (1955), which argues that—contrary to the standard view —Anglo-American relations were surprisingly cordial during this decade. Administrative problems are the theme of Charles M. Thomas, *American Neutrality in 1793: A Study in Cabinet Government* (1931). Alexander DeConde's *Entangling Alliance: Politics and Diplomacy under George Washington* (1958) is a synthesis of domestic political history and diplomatic history, somewhat critical of Washington ("Slow of mind, he took his ideas and theories, without much question, from Hamilton").

Memorandum on the Monroe Doctrine (1930) is a good factual and documentary survey, compiled by J. Reuben Clark, of the background of the Doctrine and its various applications, actual and theoretical. Edward H. Tatum Jr.'s *The United States and Europe, 1815–1823* (1936) is a monograph that likewise deals with the background of the Monroe Doctrine. Dexter Perkins is the outstanding American authority on the subject: see especially his *The Monroe Doctrine, 1823–1826* (1923). *John Quincy Adams and the Foundations of American Foreign Policy* (1949; reprinted 1956), by Samuel Flagg Bemis, is the first volume of a splendid biography which goes up to the eve of Adams' election to the presidency and which concentrates on his diplomatic career. The final chapter recapitulates the bases of American foreign policy from 1776 to 1826. (The second and last volume, *John Quincy Adams and the Union* [1956], is a work of similarly high quality, on Adams' "second career" as President and congressman.) Bemis is also the author of *Jay's Treaty* (1923) and *Pinckney's Treaty* (1926).

Among the best general surveys of territorial growth are Ray A. Billington, *Westward Expansion: A History of the American Frontier* (1949); Ralph H. Brown, *Historical Geography of the United States* (1948); Lois K. Mathews, *The Expansion of New England* (1909); Robert E. Riegel, *America Moves West* (3d ed., 1956); and

Bibliographical Note

Frederick J. Turner, *Rise of the New West, 1819–1829* (1906). Louis B. Wright's *Culture on the Moving Frontier* (1955) stresses the importance of the British heritage in bringing civilization to the West. On immigration, the classic account is Marcus L. Hansen's *The Atlantic Migration, 1607–1860* (1940). Commercial and industrial developments are ably treated in Thomas C. Cochran and William Miller, *The Age of Enterprise: A Social History of Industrial America* (1942); Edward C. Kirkland, *A History of American Economic Life* (3d ed., 1951); George R. Taylor, *The Transportation Revolution, 1815–1860* (1951), broader in scope than its title suggests; Robert G. Albion, *The Rise of New York Port [1815–60]* (1939); Louis C. Hunter, *Steamboats on the Western Rivers: An Economic and Technological History* (1949); and Victor S. Clark, *History of Manufactures in the United States,* Volume I, *1607–1860* (1929). *Men in Business* (1952) is a collection of essays in entrepreneurial history edited by William Miller, which includes one by Robert K. Lamb, "The Entrepreneur and the Community," on the activities of such New England families as the Browns and Lowells, and one by Dorothy Gregg, "John Stevens, General Entrepreneur, 1749–1838," on early steamboat enterprises in the New York area. Elva Tooker writes on *Nathan Trotter: Philadelphia Merchant, 1787–1853* (1955). On the cotton gin and Whitney's "uniformity system" in his Connecticut gun factory, see Jeannette Mirsky and Allan Nevins, *The World of Eli Whitney* (1952), and Constance McL. Green, *Eli Whitney and the Birth of American Technology* (1956). Carleton Mabee's *American Leonardo* (1943) deals with another versatile American inventor, Samuel F. B. Morse. Louis Hartz's *Economic Policy and Democratic Thought: Pennsylvania, 1776–1860* (1948) and Oscar and Mary F. Handlin's *Commonwealth: A Study of the Role of Government in the American Economy: Massachusetts, 1774–1861* (1947) convincingly uphold the thesis that, whatever the objections to control by the *national* government, *state* governments were remarkably active in stimulating and directing economic development.

Anglo-American economic relations are illuminated in Ralph W. Hidy's *The House of Baring in Anglo-American Trade and Finance* (1949) and in Norman S. Buck's *Development and Organization of Anglo-American Trade* (1925). Protectionism is lucidly presented in one old study, Orrin L. Elliott's *The Tariff Controversy in the*

The Nation Takes Shape

United States, 1789–1833 (1892), and in a more recent collection, *The Great Tariff Debate, 1820–1830* (1953), edited by George R. Taylor. The same editor, in the same admirable Amherst series, "Problems in American Civilization," examines the question of the B.U.S. in *Jackson versus Biddle—the Struggle over the Second Bank of the United States* (1949). The newest and most extended investigation of the struggle, its antecedents, and its consequences is Bray Hammond's *Banks and Politics in America from the Revolution to the Civil War* (1957). In this witty, trenchant book the author challenges the notion propagated by Arthur M. Schlesinger Jr.'s *The Age of Jackson* (1945) that the contest involved a clash between democratic ideals and capitalist practices. Biddle's own words can be studied in *The Correspondence of Nicholas Biddle . . . 1807–1844*, edited by Reginald C. McGrane (1919).

Merle Curti's *The Roots of American Loyalty* (1946), Ralph H. Gabriel's *The Course of American Democratic Thought* (2d ed., 1956), and Hans Kohn's *American Nationalism: An Interpretative Essay* (1957) analyze the formation and quality of American patriotism. So, with reference to Constitution-worship, does Frank I. Schechter in "The Early History of the Constitution," *American Political Science Review*, IX (1915), 707. Its literary manifestations are the subject of Benjamin T. Spencer's *The Quest for Nationality: An American Literary Campaign* (1957). *Nationalism and Sectionalism in America: 1775–1877* (1949) is a well-chosen collection of readings interspersed with shrewd comment by the editors, David M. Potter and Thomas G. Manning. James T. Flexner's *The Light of Distant Skies: American Painting, 1760–1835* (1954) reveals the plight of American artists torn between their homeland and Europe. John Trumbull's *Autobiography, Reminiscences, and Letters . . . from 1756 to 1841* (1841) is a firsthand expression of their difficulties. There are some perceptive remarks on American attitudes to nature in Perry Miller's *Errand into the Wilderness* (1956). The patriotic activities of the "Brahmin Rebel" George Bancroft are recounted in Russel B. Nye's biography (1944), and those of Noah Webster in Harry R. Warfel, *Schoolmaster to America* (1936). Warfel has also edited *The Letters of Noah Webster* (1953). Thomas P. Abernethy's *The Burr Conspiracy* (1954), the latest though probably not the last word on that mysterious affair, is somewhat more sympathetic than

Bibliographical Note

the outright condemnation by Henry Adams. Charles S. Sydnor's *The Development of Southern Sectionalism, 1819–1848* (1948) is an excellent contribution to the "History of the South" series. See also Charles H. Ambler, *Sectionalism in Virginia from 1776 to 1861* (1910); Jesse T. Carpenter, *The South as a Conscious Minority, 1789–1861* (1930); Clement Eaton, *Freedom of Thought in the Old South* (1940, reprinted 1951); John H. Franklin, *The Militant South, 1800–1861* (1956); Glover Moore, *The Missouri Controversy, 1819–1821* (1953); and Kenneth M. Stampp, *The Peculiar Institution: Slavery in the Ante-Bellum South* (1956). Albert F. Simpson, "The Political Significance of Slave Representation, 1787–1821," *Journal of Southern History*, VII (1941), 315, shows how worried New Englanders were by what they regarded as southern political dominance. There is some unfamiliar material in Arthur A. Ekirch Jr.'s *The Idea of Progress in America, 1815–1860* (1944), which includes a chapter on "The Defense of Social Stability."

The intricate issues of conservatism and democracy have given rise to a large and growing bibliography. For the early days, what might be called the Republican case is documented by Eugene P. Link, *Democratic-Republican Societies, 1790–1800* (1942); Stuart G. Brown, *The First Republicans* (1954); Leland D. Baldwin's *Whiskey Rebels* (1939); two studies of the Alien and Sedition Acts, John C. Miller's *Crisis in Freedom* (1951) and James M. Smith's *Freedom's Fetters* (1956); *The Journal of William Maclay*, edited by Edgar S. Maclay (1890); and Charles Warren's *Jacobin and Junto: Or, Early American Politics as Viewed in the Diary of Dr. Nathaniel Ames, 1758–1822* (1931). The doctor's Federàlist brother's opinions are gathered in *The Works of Fisher Ames* (2 vols., 1854).

The Federalist position is made clear, too, in Stephen G. Kurtz's *The Presidency of John Adams* (1957), an able analysis of Adams' great gifts and even greater difficulties; Manning J. Dauer, *The Adams Federalists* (1953), which except for some refinements has in the author's opinion "confirmed earlier interpretations, especially those of [Charles A.] Beard"; and Morton Borden, *The Federalism of James A. Bayard* (1955), which shows that Bayard, though emotionally "Federalist," was bound by no very strict ties of party allegiance. John Adams' own opinions are set out forcibly in his collected *Works* (10 vols., 1850–56). The annotations to the books he read are admirably reconstructed by Zoltán Haraszti in *John Adams and the Prophets of Progress* (1952). Joseph Charles's three essays on *The Origins of the American Party System* (1956) contain some acute speculations on politics in the 1790's; and see Noble E. Cunningham Jr.'s *The Jeffersonian Republicans: The Formation of Party Organization, 1789–1801* (1957).

There are a number of valuable biographies or autobiographies relating to men of the time. Samuel Eliot Morison's *Life and Letters of Harrison Gray Otis, Federalist: 1756–1848* (2 vols., 1913) is one of the best; and worthy to set beside it is Raymond Walters Jr.'s *Albert Gallatin: Jeffersonian Financier and Diplomat* (1957). The divided aims of such New England men of letters as Joel Barlow and Timothy Dwight are perceptively discussed in Leon Howard's *The Connecticut Wits* (1943). There is a graceful life of the New York Conservative *James Kent* by John T. Horton (1939). Conservatives who have written their own memoirs include Charles Biddle, *Autobiography, 1745–1821* (1883); Samuel G. Goodrich, *Recollections of a Lifetime* (2 vols., 1856); and, in edited form, the *Life and Letters of Joseph Story* (2 vols., 1851), and Elkanah Watson's *Men and Times of the Revolution* (1856).

Some important work has been done on individual states, the study of which often tells us more than do broad statements about the national political scene. The interactions of state and national politics, for instance, are well brought out in Harry M. Tinkcom's *Republicans and Federalists in Pennsylvania, 1789–1801* (1950). See also James A. Kehl's *Ill Feeling in the Era of Good Feeling: Western Pennsylvania Political Battles, 1815–1825* (1956); Thomas P. Abernethy's *From Frontier to Plantation in Tennessee: A Study in Frontier Democracy* (1932), which contends that "a group of . . . unscrupulous practitioners of the art of fooling the people put [Andrew Jackson] over as the anointed prophet of the new order. . . . He was the figurehead rather than . . . the leader of the democratic movement which bears his name"—a view substantiated to some extent by Charles G. Sellers Jr., "Jackson Men with Feet of Clay," *American Historical Review*, LXII (1957), 537; Harry R. Stevens, *The Early Jackson Party in Ohio* (1957); and Arthur B. Darling, *Political Changes in Massachusetts, 1824–1848* (1925). All of these bear witness to the intricacy of local issues and the blurring of broader divi-

Bibliographical Note

sions. So does Glyndon G. Van Deusen ("Some Aspects of Whig Thought and Theory in the Jacksonian Period," *American Historical Review*, LXIII [1958], 305), who concludes that on the national level, "the political conflicts of the Jacksonian period were fought more often with a view to gaining control of the government than out of devotion to diametrically opposed political and social ideals." This view dissents somewhat from that put forward in such older interpretations as Dixon R. Fox's *The Decline of Aristocracy in the Politics of New York* (1919), and Walter R. Fee's *The Transition from Aristocracy to Democracy in New Jersey, 1789–1829* (1933).

While at times he comes close to Arthur M. Schlesinger Jr.'s view of the era as one displaying marked ideological differences, nevertheless William N. Chambers' biography of Thomas Hart Benton (*Old Bullion Benton* [1956]) stresses the "Arcadia-Enterprise" ambivalence of Jackson and his followers. Benton is also the subject of E. B. Smith's *Magnificent Missourian* (1957). The theme is emphasized in another exemplary biography, Charles G. Sellers Jr.'s *James K. Polk, Jacksonian: 1795–1843* (1957), which sees Polk as "plunging headlong into the exploitation . . . of a bounteous environment, yet drawn almost as powerfully back toward the simplicity and virtue of a half-imagined agrarian past." John W. Ward's *Andrew Jackson: Symbol for an Age* (1955) is a sensitive portrait of Jackson as the embodiment in myth of his era in America—a threefold myth of "nature," "providence," and "will." In another brilliant study, closer in interpretation to the actualities of the American political scene, Marvin Meyers explains the various nuances of *The Jacksonian Persuasion* (1957). I have learned much from his book. There is both amusement and instruction to be derived, too, from contemporary political reminiscences, among which Thurlow Weed's *Autobiography* (1883), edited by his daughter Harriet A. Weed, stands high. The best life of John C. Calhoun is that by Charles M. Wiltse (3 vols., 1944–51; the first two are relevant for the period). In addition to the older, substantial studies of Henry Clay and Daniel Webster there are short recent biographies by Clement Eaton (1957) and Richard N. Current (1955), respectively. There is room for a new investigation of Martin Van Buren; in the meantime, Holmes Alexander's biography, *The American Talleyrand* (1935), is readable though too sweeping in criticism.

The Nation Takes Shape

Alexis de Tocqueville's profoundly important *Democracy in America* is available in many editions. The best of these, in translation, is by Phillips Bradley (1945; reprinted in paperback edition 1954), who adds a long critical essay. The book should be read in conjunction with George W. Pierson's *Tocqueville and Beaumont in America* (1938), an exhaustive inquiry which suggests among other things that "Equality in America" would have been a more accurate rendering of the title. The accounts of other contemporary observers, American and European, are too numerous to mention individually. The following are helpful guides to or anthologies of this abundant material: Durand Echeverria, *Mirage in the West: A History of the French Image of American Society to 1815* (1957); Oscar Handlin (ed.), *This Was America* (1949); Jane L. Mesick, *The English Traveller in America, 1785–1835* (1922); Frank Monaghan, *French Travellers in the United States, 1765–1932* (1933); Allan Nevins (ed.), *America through British Eyes* (1948); Robert E. Spiller, *The American in England during the First Half Century of Independence* (1926); and Warren S. Tryon (ed.), *A Mirror for Americans: Life and Manners in the United States, 1790–1870, as Recorded by American Travelers* (3 vols., 1952). James Fenimore Cooper's disenchanted *The American Democrat* (1838) has been reprinted (1956) in a paperback edition with a knowledgeable introduction by Robert E. Spiller. A special issue of *New York History* (1954) was devoted to a reappraisal of Cooper, with some emphasis on his significance as a social critic.

Important Dates

1789   George Washington inaugurated as first President of the United States (John Adams Vice-President), April 30

1791   First Bank of the United States chartered, February
Vermont joins Union as fourteenth state, March 4
Report on manufactures submitted to Congress by Alexander Hamilton, December 5

1792   Kentucky joins Union as fifteenth state, June 1

1793   President Washington inaugurated for second term (John Adams again Vice-President), March 4
France declares war on Britain, Spain, and Holland, February
Neutrality proclamation issued by Washington, April 22

1794   Whiskey "Rebellion" in western Pennsylvania, July–November
General Anthony Wayne defeats Ohio Indians at Fallen Timbers, August 20

1795   Senate ratifies Jay's Treaty with Britain, June 24
Pinckney's Treaty with Spain signed, October 27

1796   Tennessee becomes sixteenth state, June 1
Washington's Farewell Address published, September 17

1797   John Adams inaugurated President (Thomas Jefferson Vice-President), March 4

The Nation Takes Shape

1798   Alien and Sedition Acts (in force until March, 1801), June–July

       Kentucky and Virginia resolutions, opposing Alien and Sedition Acts, November–December

1800   Federal government moves from Philadelphia to Washington, D.C., June

       By Treaty of San Ildefonso, Spain cedes Louisiana to France, October

1801   Jefferson inaugurated President (Aaron Burr Vice-President) after electoral deadlock, March 4

1802   U.S. Military Academy formally opened at West Point, N.Y., July 4

1803   Ohio admitted as seventeenth state, February 19

       U.S. takes formal possession of Louisiana (sale by France negotiated in April), December 20

1804   Lewis and Clark expedition sets out from St. Louis to explore Louisiana Purchase and Far West, May

       Alexander Hamilton fatally wounded in duel with Aaron Burr, July 11

1805   Jefferson re-inaugurated as President (George Clinton Vice-President), March 4

1806   Non-Importation Act passed against Britain (suspended December, 1806, not invoked again until December, 1808), April 18

1807   Act of Congress prohibiting importation of slaves after January 1, 1808, March 2

       Chesapeake-Leopard incident, June 22

       Aaron Burr acquitted on charge of treason, September 1

       Embargo Act becomes law (replaced March, 1809, by Non-Intercourse Act), December 22

1809   James Madison inaugurated President (Vice-President George Clinton), March 4

1810   Annexation of West Florida, October 27

Important Dates

1811   Success over Indians gained by William Henry Harrison at Tippecanoe (Indiana), November 7

1812   Louisiana becomes eighteenth state, April 8
Declaration of war on Great Britain, June 18

1813   President Madison re-inaugurated (Vice-President Elbridge Gerry), March 4
American naval victory on Lake Erie, September 10
Andrew Jackson's campaign against Creek Indians (Alabama), November–March, 1814

1814   British capture and burning of Washington, D.C., August
American naval victory on Lake Champlain, September 11
War of 1812 ended by Treaty of Ghent, December 24

1815   Battle of New Orleans, January 8

1816   Second Bank of the United States chartered, April 10
Indiana enters Union as nineteenth state, December 11

1817   James Monroe inaugurated as President (Daniel D. Tompkins Vice-President), March 4
Mississippi becomes twentieth state, December 10

1818   Jackson's Seminole campaign in East Florida, April–May
Illinois becomes twenty-first state of Union, December 3

1819   Cession of East Florida by Spain (Adams-Onís Treaty), February
Alabama becomes twenty-second state of Union, December 14

1820   Passage of Missouri Compromise (slavery excluded from the Louisiana Purchase north of the line 36° 30′), March 3
Maine becomes twenty-third state of Union, March 15

1821   James Monroe re-inaugurated President (D. D. Tompkins again Vice-President), March 5
Missouri admitted to Union as twenty-fourth state, August 10

1823   "Monroe Doctrine" outlined in President's annual message to Congress, December 2

1825   John Quincy Adams inaugurated President (John C. Calhoun Vice-President), March 4

1825　Erie Canal officially opened from Buffalo to Albany, October 26

1828　"Tariff of Abominations" passed by Congress, April–May

1829　Andrew Jackson inaugurated President (Vice-President John C. Calhoun), March 4

1830　Maysville Road veto by Jackson, May 27

1831　Nat Turner slave insurrection in Southampton County, Virginia, August

1832　Veto by Jackson of bill to recharter the Bank of the United States, July 10
　　　Termination of Black Hawk War, August
　　　South Carolina Ordinance of Nullification, November 24

1833　Jackson re-inaugurated President (Martin Van Buren Vice-President), March 4

1835　Outbreak of Second Seminole War in Florida (not finally terminated until 1843), November

1836　Texan declaration of independence (conceded by Mexico in May, after siege of the Alamo in March and Battle of San Jacinto in April; concession subsequently repudiated by Mexico), March 2
　　　Arkansas admitted to Union as twenty-fifth state, June 15

1837　Michigan admitted to Union as twenty-sixth state, January 26
　　　Republic of Texas formally recognized by U.S., March 3
　　　Martin Van Buren inaugurated President (Vice-President Richard M. Johnson), March 4
　　　Suspension of specie payment by New York banks, followed by severe economic depression, May 10

Index

[Italicized references are bibliographical]

Index

Congregationalism, 78, 91, 156, 184

Connecticut, 73, 113, 118, 138, 144, 156, 159, 160, 175–76

Constitution, federal: making of, 11–12, 24, 150–51, 154; working-out of, 11–38 *passim;* worship of, 39, 123, 126–27, 135, 173

Continental Congress, 12, 137

Cooper, James Fenimore (1789–1851), 136, 168–69, 176–77, 184, *210*

Copley, John S. (1738?–1815), 189

Cotton: cultivation, 82–84, 85, 101, 142; manufactures, 82, 101, 118–19

Cowpens, Battle of, 125, 131–32

Crawford, William H. (1772–1834), 38, 162

Crèvecœur, Michel-Guillaume Jean de (1735–1813), 155

Crockett, Davy (David) (1786–1836), 158

Cuba, 43

Cumberland Gap, 79

Davis, Jefferson (1808–89), 77

Debt: imprisonment for, 153, 159; national, funding of, 3, 25–27; state debts, assumption of, 25–27

Decatur, Stephen (1779–1820), 133–34

Declaration of Independence, 6, 39, 123, 150, 153, 199

Deere, John (1804–86), 182

Delaware estuary, 104

Democratic party, 27–28, 153–80 *passim, 208–9*

Democratic Review (founded 1837), 2–4, 7, 9–10

Dennie, Joseph (1768–1812), 155

Depressions, economic: of 1819, 82; of 1837, 96, 112–13, 121, 166, 214

Detroit, Fort, 42, 75

Dickens, Charles, 188

Disraeli, Benjamin, 170

Douglas, Stephen A. (1813–61), 77

Dwight, Timothy (1752–1817), 118, *208*

Eagle, American, as national symbol, 126

Edwards, Ninian (1775–1833), 178–79

Embargo, 56–58, 212

Emerson, Ralph Waldo (1803–82), 91, 182–83, 184, 191, 193

Episcopalianism, 160, 171, 185

Erie, Lake, 79; Battle of, 59, 131, 213

Erie Canal, 87, 106–7, 214

"Essex Junto," 144, 146, 151

Evans, Nathaniel (1742–67), 188

Evans, Oliver (1755–1819), 118

Everett, Edward (1794–1865), 108, 110

Exports, 3, 96–97, 101–2, 118

Fall River (Mass.), 118–19

Fallen Timbers, Battle of, 75, 211

Farewell Address, Washington's, 21, 30–31, 43–44, 65, 128, 143, 211

Federalism, 8, 24, 27–28, 35, 45, 49, 53, 60, 78, 135, 144, 150–51, 160–61, 170–80, 194, *207–8*

Federalist, The, 15, 28

Fink, Mike (1770?–1823?), 103

Fish, Carl R., *154*

Flint, Timothy (1780–1840), 99

Florida: Spanish, 52, 58, 62, 70, 140; Territory, 38, 85

Fourth of July celebrations, 39, 123–24, 126–27, 144

France, relations of, with United States, 40–42, 44, 46, 48–50, 51–53, 56–58, 67, 139

Franklin, Benjamin (1706–90), 1, 6, 11, 12, 126, 155

Freemasonry, 159

Freneau, Philip (1752–1832), 129–30

Fulton, Robert (1765–1815), 86, 104, 190

217

Index

Index

THE CHICAGO HISTORY OF AMERICAN CIVILIZATION

Daniel J. Boorstin, Editor

Edmund S. Morgan, *The Birth of the Republic: 1763–89*

Marcus Cunliffe, *The Nation Takes Shape: 1789–1837*

John Hope Franklin, *Reconstruction: After the Civil War*

Samuel P. Hays, *The Response to Industrialism: 1885–1914*

William E. Leuchtenburg, *The Perils of Prosperity: 1914–32*

Dexter Perkins, *The New Age of Franklin Roosevelt: 1932–45*

Herbert Agar, *The Price of Power: America since 1945*

* * *

Robert H. Bremner, *American Philanthropy*

*Harry L. Coles, *The War of 1812*

Richard M. Dorson, *American Folklore*

John Tracy Ellis, *American Catholicism*

Nathan Glazer, *American Judaism*

William T. Hagan, *American Indians*

Winthrop S. Hudson, *American Protestantism*

Maldwyn Allen Jones, *American Immigration*

Robert G. McCloskey, *The American Supreme Court*

Howard H. Peckham, *The War for Independence: A Military History*

Howard H. Peckham, *The Colonial Wars: 1689–1762*

Henry Pelling, *American Labor*

Charles P. Roland, *The Confederacy*

Otis A. Singletary, *The Mexican War*

John F. Stover, *American Railroads*

*Bernard A. Weisberger, *The American Newspaperman*

* Available in cloth only. All other books published in both cloth and paperback editions.